ELECTRICITY OF THE MIND

The Anomalist no.14: A Nonfiction Anthology

Ian Simmons, Editor

ANOMALIST BOOKS
San Antonio * New York

An Original Publication of ANOMALIST BOOKS

ELECTRICITY OF THE MIND
Copyright © 2010 by Patrick Huyghe and Dennis Stacy
ISBN: 1933665394

Cover image design courtesy of Thomas Thamm/North100.com

Book design by Seale Studios

For information, go to anomalistbooks.com, or write to: Anomalist
Books, 5150 Broadway #108, San Antonio, TX 78209

To John Keel, John Michell, and Ken Campbell,
who passed away during the production of this volume and without
whom our understanding of the fortean would be much diminished.

CONTENTS

THE TOPOGRAPHY OF THE DAMNED
BY THEO PAIJMANS

We live in an age with certain technological benefits that Charles Fort could only have dreamt of. In the slipstream of the digital revolution many newspapers have been digitized. The result is that those hunting for Fortean anomalies can search through millions of 18th, 19th, and 20th century newspaper pages from the United States, Australia, Canada, England, and New Zealand. There is more good news: there are more digital newspaper archives in countries worldwide, all with varying degrees of accessibility, quantity of content, and user friendly interfaces.

From the comfort of our homes we can now search through many more newspaper pages than Fort read during his entire life. We see the results of our search queries in the blink of an eye as compared to Fort's time. Unique as a tool and impressive as this is, the millions of digitized newspaper pages are still but a fraction of what has been published since the advent of the newspaper as the premier chronicler of our culture. The digitization processes, welcome as they are, are in their infancy. What renders Fort's work pioneering is that he was able to use a vast array of sources to chart entire areas of anomalies not brought together before, well before the advent of the internet with its digitized, fully searchable documents and powerful search engines. Fort coined terms for puzzling events in a time when he had to physically wade through page after page, hoping that he would not miss those, say, five little lines in the smallest of typefaces, tucked somewhere at the bottom half of this or that dusty publication, or needing to resort to card file indexes in forbidding cabinets and with no Fortean classification systems in place. That was the way in the pre-internet, pre *Book of the Damned* era.

These days, our dearly beloved anomalies are relatively easy uncovered, as the digital newspaper archives harbor digitized newspapers from many countries, states, cities, and localities in searchable databases. Since we can virtually type in any keyword, including search strings such as "fish falls," the question arises where and how we would have begun had not Fort collected and named the many strange events in the Topography of the Damned to clear a path before us with his books as a guide.

Fort's oeuvre is still a primary source for later books on weird events. Apart from George Eberhart's important *Geo-Bibliography of Anomalies*, attempts to approach his Damned Data with a different research objective in mind are very scarce, aside from the study and interpretation of the anomaly event, or its geographical location. The entirely new approach presented here, and the primary topic of this paper, is the geographical distribution and dispersion of the accounts of the damned data through time and how they march through the various newspapers, ultimately on an international scale. And, by tracing these trails, we are able to draw new conclusions in regards to Fort's oeuvre and sometimes even find surprising solutions to, and fresh interpretations of, these puzzling anomalies. This important and entirely new field of study has been made possible through the digitization process. The study of the publishing history of anomalous events in the 19th and 20th century newspapers helps in charting cultural influences, the rise and development of folkloric motifs, and the evolution and classification of the anomalous events themselves. Moreover, realizing how dependent Forteana is on the existence of sources and references of what in themselves are strange enough tales, the various digital newspaper projects enable us to at least begin to form an idea of the quantities of source materials involved, an aspect that was largely unresearchable in the analog age.

In the reporting on a specific anomaly over a certain period of time we can also attempt to unravel the inevitable mutation that sets in, the gradual formation of the legend that provides new detail. This evolving context may help in tracing an anomaly back to its ultimate bibliographical roots and original sources. And who knows, perhaps we even may formulate new interpretations that lead toward more insight or avenues of research. An example is the reporting on the Beaman Monster, which for decades has terrorized the Beaman neighborhood near Sedalia, Missouri. It has its origins in a number of strange sightings in the late 1950s. There was something unusual going on in Beaman, as the *Daily Capital News*, the newspaper from Jefferson City, Missouri, reported in its August 8, 1959 edition. A surprised witness had seen "a mother monkey with three young ones" cross a road in Beaman. The mother was five feet tall, the young ones a foot and a half to two feet. The trooper who went to investigate offered as possible explanation the escape of "a bunch of monkeys" from their cage during a tornado that had struck the Missouri State Fair in 1952. They were never recaptured. "But I can't figure out how they could have withstood the common winters," the trooper commented. The year before a creature described as a gorilla had been sighted in the area, and there had been sightings of a wild man "eating live chickens" and a bear.(1)

Half a century after the initial events, in February 2008, the Missouri newspaper *Constitution-Tribune* from Chillicothe recounted how the Beaman Monster phenomenon had not died down. "People have told tales of the Beaman Monster for more than 100 years, although no evidence of the creature exists," it reported. Now the monster included, according to one eyewitness, "a wolf-shaped creature," and one story, recalled by an 81-year-old resident as told by his father to him, had it that the origins of the Beaman Monster could be traced to 1904, emerging from then current tales of an escaped 12-foot-tall gorilla from a wrecked circus train that year.(2) According to an eyewitness who had seen it in the 1990s when about ten years old and riding in the bed of a pickup truck "a wolf-shaped creature came out of the woods and began to run alongside the vehicle. It wasn't quite animalistic... It's hard to explain unless you've seen it."(3)

In her book *The Beast Of Bray Road: Tailing Wisconsin's Werewolf*, published in 2003, Linda Godfrey recounted sightings of a wolf-like creature around Elkhorn, Wisconsin, in the early 1990s. Her book, her earlier newspaper articles on the creature, or the nationwide coverage in various newspapers that followed in the wake of her original reports might each have influenced the description of a wolf-like creature stalking the area in the Beaman Monster saga. Yet the late 1970s to the early 1990s was a period when stories of sightings of strange man-wolves were published in newspapers in various parts of America. Sometimes these involved hoaxes and pranks of bored, dressed-up teenagers who were out to scare a community, and sometimes they were puzzling accounts of improbable creatures. All in all this is suggestive of a nationwide flap, and it is also possible that the eyewitness account of the wolf-like creature at Beaman can be seen in the light of these occurrences.

Tentative solutions to cold cases
Sometimes we can even solve one of those little mysteries that profusely clutter the Fortean canon by retracing Fort's and others' sources in the digital archives. Writes Fort in *Lo!*: "A field, somewhere near, Salem, Va., in the year 1885 – and that in this field there was a suction. In the New York Sun, April 25, 1885, it is said that Isaac Martin, a young farmer, living near Salem, Va., had gone into a field, to work, and that he had disappeared. It is said that in this region there had been

other mysterious disappearances."(4) Fort errs on his source as it was not printed in the *New York Sun* but in *The Sun*, a newspaper from Baltimore, Maryland, where I located it: "Isaac Martin, a young farmer, near Salem, Va., left his home Wednesday and went into the fields to work, and nothing has been heard of him since. This is the second case of mysterious disappearance in that immediate neighborhood in the last two weeks."(5) Contrary to Fort there is mention of just one disappearance before Martin vanished, taking away some of the luster and mystique that surrounds Fort's summary. Farmers walking into fields and suddenly disappearing – this has been a potent if untrue lure in Forteana ever since Ambrose Bierce's tales of vanishing men and the later, spurious accounts of the sudden disappearances of Oliver Lerch one night in South Bend, Indiana, and of David Lang, on a clear day in a field in Tennessee.

But we find the sad answer to this riddle of what befell Isaac Martin in a small announcement in a Georgia newspaper of May, 1885: "Isaac Martin, a young farmer near Salem, who mysteriously disappeared over six weeks ago, and for whom an exhaustive search was made, was unaccounted for until Saturday, when his body was found hanging to a tree not far from his home."(6) In our Fortean universe, the solution poses another riddle, often encountered with the finding of the remains of missing persons; notwithstanding an exhaustive search that, we may assume, would also have included the area in the vicinity of his home, his body, all the time hanging in a tree "not far from his home," was not found for five weeks.

Loren Coleman writes in the second edition of his *Mothman and Other Curious Encounters* that was published in 2002: "During the 1960s and 1970s I dug into the back issues of the Louisville, Kentucky, *Courier-Journal* and discovered a gem that has kept me pondering its meaning for decades. The interesting little item appeared in the October 24, 1878 issue. A 'Wild Man of the Woods' was captured, allegedly, in Tennessee, and then placed on exhibit in Louisville. The creature was described as being six feet, five inches tall, and having eyes twice the normal size. His body was 'covered with fish scales.'"(7)

Unfortunately, the *Courier-Journal* is not currently digitized. Researching this particular item, I located it in several other newspapers from various states (8) indicating that the account was published nationwide. I also discovered the solution to this Lovecraftian description of a mysterious Deep One, in an Iowa newspaper, the *Waterloo Courier*. Quoting the *Courier-Journal*, it published in its December 1878 issue the opinion of a Dr. L.P. Yandell, who was "among the medical men who took a look at the man-fish... He gives in the *Medical News* the following interesting statement in regards to the wonder: 'A short time since the Tennessee and Kentucky newspapers contained a startling account of a wild man lately captured, with great difficulty, in the Cumberland Mountains. He was six feet ten inches high, extraordinarily fleet of foot and excessively savage. He fed chiefly on raw fish, which he captured without artificial aid. He spent much of his time in the water, and after being captured he had to be frequently bathed. He was covered with shining scales, like those of a fish. His hands and feet were webbed like the feet of water-fowls, so the newspaper accounts, with many embellishments, ran. It is scarcely necessary to say that much of this story was only showman's talk, uttered to attract the attention of the curious and credulous public.... Amongst others I visited the merman; but before seeing the case I had diagnosed it as one of the *ichthyosis*, and a single glance was sufficient to verify the correctness of my conjecture. The man-fish presents a most magnificent example of the form of *ichthyosis*, or fish-skin disease, called *ichthyosis serpentine*, or serpent skin, and his general effect is more that of a serpent than of a fish. But upon different parts of his body may be found nearly all the varieties of *ichthyosis*... About his joints the skin is loose and wrinkled, hanging in folds, and the scales are large, suggesting the skin of a lizard or alligator about their limbs and belly. His arms and legs remind one of the skin of the buffalo perch, the carp or other large fish... There seems to be an absolute absence of fat, and the man is shrunken and withered, of a dead ashen-gray appearance, except here and there, where he is brownish or blackish... Though only about fifty years of age, he impresses one as a very old man. The skin of the face is red and shining, and tightly drawn about the cheeks... In some cases his scales are silvery, in others dark... His hair is very thin and dead looking... he is considerably over six feet in height, and a man of a low order of intelligence. He is married and the father of several children, none of whom, fortunately, inherit his malady..."(9)

Accounts of anomalies appear much more frequently, and nationwide, than was previously thought of or considered. What this means for the gradual creation of a proto-Fortean mindset in the early American newspaper reader, and what influence this might have had in subsequent reportings, is perhaps illustrated by the coverage of the strange event at Copiapó in 1868.

The Copiapó Flying Anomaly

The Copiapó event is a puzzling account that since its inception in Fort's *Lo!* has found its way in several other Fortean and ufological books. In 1868, according to the *Zoologist* of July 1868, startled laborers of a mine saw, writes Fort, "something that was seen in the sky, near Copiapo, Chile – a construction that carried lights, and was propelled by a noisy motor – or 'a gigantic bird; eyes wide open and shining like burning coals; covered with immense scales, which clashed together with a metallic sound.'"(10)

The Copiapó flying anomaly has a rare quality to it. Not only is the event itself bizarre, but so is the single source that Fort quotes, and that, if not quoting Fort as source, is usually referred to by later authors citing this case. Yet before it was printed in the *Zoologist*, it had found its way in various American newspapers since its initial publication in Copiapó's newspaper *El Constituyente* of March 18, 1868.(11) So far I have located the account in eight American newspapers from various states, where it was published between May and June 1868 (12), indicating a nationwide distribution and making the *Zoologist* entry a relatively late one.

The original account, as it was published in the American newspapers, is much longer than Fort's summary: "Yesterday, about five o'clock P.M., when everyone had finished work at this mine, Garin Mine, and the workmen in a group were awaiting their evening meal, we saw coming through the air a gigantic bird, which at first sight we supposed to be a cloud surrounded by the atmosphere, and divided from its companions by a chance current of air.

"As the object in question came nearer, filling us with a very natural feeling of surprise, we were able to note that it was an unknown creature of the air – the *roc* of the *Thousand and One Nights* perhaps, or possibly a Leviathan of the deserts. From whence did it come? To where was it going? Its direction was from northeast to southwest; its flight rapid and in a direct line. On passing a short distance and over our heads, we were able to note the rare structure of its body. Its great wings were clothed with a brown plumage; the head of the monster was in shape similar to that of the grasshopper, with enormous eyes wide opened and brilliant as stars, and covered with something like hair or bristles; the body, lengthening itself out like that of a serpent, was covered with brilliant scales, which emitted metallic sounds as the strange animal moved itself along.

"Surprise resolved itself into fear among the workmen in the presence of such a strange phenomenon. The whole stock or ornithological science possessed by the good miners was in vain exhausted to find the name and qualities of the strange bird which had just passed without leaving a sign. Some assert that in those moments they perceived a detestable smell, like that given out by arsenic on being burned, others that their senses were not offended by any unusual odor. The superstitious believe that it is the devil in person they have just seen pass, while others recollect having been witness, some years ago, in the same place, of the passage of a similar monstrous bird.

"As the whole affair is in the extreme curious, we have thought it our duty to communicate it to you, withholding all the useless comment, for the truth is that we cannot explain satisfactorily to ourselves what we have seen for the first and probably the last time in our lives. Can it be possible that in the desert or the Cordilleras, Nature pleases to give life to these monstrosities, and rears them in solitude for many years, and when they have attained sufficient strength they commence their flight through space, and the earth guards their skeletons to the confusion of sages who on meeting them believe they have found antediluvian remains?"(13)

This account was published in a Wisconsin newspaper, the *Milwaukee Daily Sentinel,* and was "translated from *El Ferro Carril* of Santiago, Chili, March 27" as the newspaper stated, indicating that it made the rounds of South American newspapers as well. In the account there is no reference or allusion to a motor or engine, possibly Fort interpreted the descriptions of a burning smell as such. Moreover, Fort has emphasized a mechanical aspect in his summary that is not entirely there in the original account, by writing about a "construction that carried lights" and alluding to a motor and the metallic sounds it made. The most interesting detail that emerges though is that "some years before" a similar phenomenon had occurred there – a fact that Fort for some reason failed to mention. Before Fort rediscovered this strange account in the *Zoologist,* many 19th century North and South Americans read it in many newspapers. In what way this account might have shaped later reports on similar aerial anomalies may be found in two of the earliest accounts of anomalous flying men over American cities. (14) Both were published in 1880, and we find in both the same elements that hint at the existence of a mechanical aspect, as if these creatures have stepped out of a strange world existing on the crossroads of mechanical structures and biological entities. In July 1880, two men from Louisville saw "'high up in the air... the appearance of a man surrounded by machinery' which he seemed to be working with his feet and hands..." The eyewitnesses could see "the delicate outlines of machinery, but the object was too high up to make out its exact construction." The account was published in the *Courier-Journal* of Louisville, suggestively headed "A Flying Machine."(15) And thus the flying anomaly that cavorted over Coney Island in September that year, described as "a man with bat's wings and improved frog's legs," of a "deep black color," and with a "cruel and determined expression" on his face must have been "a man fitted with practicable wings... Some one has solved the problem of aerial navigation by inventing wings..." The account also refers to the Louisville incident: "About a month ago an object of precisely the same nature was seen in the air over St. Louis... A little later it was seen by various Kentucky persons as it flew across the State." Fort also quotes this 1880 account. As with the Copiapó account, either Fort or his source, the *New York Times,* is always used by later writers.

But as in the case of the Copiapó anomaly, the Coney Island Flying Man tale was published in other American newspapers. Thus far I have located it in three different newspapers (16) from Massachusetts, Arkansas, and North Carolina, and I suspect it was published in other newspaper as well. Surprisingly, I did not locate it in the *Brooklyn Daily Eagle* where one would have expected it, as it featured other news of Coney Island. I have not been able to find an account of a strange flying anomaly over St. Louis in 1880. In 1948, St. Louis was plagued by the appearance of a flying anomaly that usually was described as a giant bird, although a St. Louis policeman likened it to a "witch flying across the sky."(17) The sightings lasted from the first week of April to the end of May but may have started as early as January that year. The reference in the 1880 Flying Man of Coney Island account, however, indicates that St. Louis has in fact had a much longer tradition of flying things seen in the sky, one going back to the 19th century.

Reading the 1880 accounts, Fort's attention clearly was drawn towards their strange mechanical details. They not only add to the strangeness, partially explaining his emphasis on the alleged machine-like aspects in his summary of the Copiapó event, but these details sit well within Fort's canon, where his writings about "super constructions" and immense artificial things that travel through the vast distances of space and the absolute elsewhere conjure up some of the most enduring images in his work. It is here that Fort presents the most disconcerting idea in his oeuvre. If the anomalies that parade in endless streams out of his books are not natural phenomena but artificial ones, and clearly not man-made, there must be another dimension, another sphere of existence where its secret inhabitants indulge themselves in treating mankind as, to quote Fort, "property."

International reporting on Fortean phenomena

"Very largely we shall concern ourselves with enormous fiery objects that have either plunged into the ocean or risen from the ocean," writes Fort in his *The Book of the Damned*. Among the many examples that he cites of luminous wheels, luminous bodies rising from the sea or hurtling through the skies, Fort tells of "...an object, described as 'a large ball of fire,' seen to rise from the sea, near Cape Race. We are told that it rose to a height of fifty feet, and then advanced close to the ship, then moving away, remaining visible about five minutes..."(18)

I have not been able to locate the account in the American newspapers, but when scanning several 19th century Dutch newspapers for Fortean items of interest, I found that the incident that had occurred in 1887 was published at the beginning of the following year in the Netherlands, Europe. This indicates a new layer of interest for study; the international reporting of Fortean events. Usually far removed from the actual or alleged occurrences, and owing to cultural differences between America and Europe, for instance, these international accounts present interesting comparative materials.

Thus far I have located the item on the anomalous sighting at Cape Race in two Dutch newspapers, the *Texelse Courant* and *Nieuwe Amersfoortsche Courant*, in their March 1888 editions. As they differ somewhat from on another, each providing us with new details, and as Fort is terse in his summary, my translations of both accounts follow: "A rare aerial phenomenon was recently observed by captain Moore of the English steamer *Siberian* when he was in the vicinity of Newfoundland, about 10 sea miles off Cape Race. He saw then at midnight – it was November 12 – with a strong wind a big fireball rising up out of the sea to a height of approximately 15 feet, and against the direction of the wind, coursing straight towards the ship. The fireball then changed course and moved parallel to the ship for about 1.5 sea miles, when about 2 minutes later it again took on another course and disappeared. Captain Moore says that he had observed such a phenomenon before at Cape Race and he considered it a sign of storm from the East and South-East.

"The Hydrographic Bureau in Washington, having submitted the above, adds to that: the phenomenon described here is one of the rarest and hard to explain forms of lightning. A fireball floats slowly through the air without fixed course to sometimes explode with tremendous force, at other times bursting in apart with an explosion in the air. People on land have observed that these fireballs, when they strike the ground, make a hole of more than 30 feet diameter and reappear a short distance away. Although the phenomenon itself is not in doubt there still has not been found a sufficient explanation."(19)

The *Nieuwe Amersfoortsche Courant* presented the account two weeks later, with different wording: "The captain of the British steamer *Siberia* recently observed, not far from Newfoundland, at 10 sea miles of Cape Race, a strange phenomenon. He saw, close to midnight, and with heavy weather, a fireball ascending from the sea which floated for a few seconds 4 meters above the sea, and subsequently disappeared. The captain had seen such a phenomenon before in these parts and thought of it as an omen of storm. The Hydrographic Bureau in Washington called it 'one of the most rare and most difficult to explain electrical phenomena.'" The fireball, it further states, "usually ascends slowly in the air and explodes with a thunderous sound. People have also seen such fireballs on the mainland, where they usually fall to the ground and create a hole of ten meters in diameter, to surface again at another place."(20)

News of the great airship wave of 1896-1897 reached Dutch newspapers, too, as this account published in the *Nieuwe Amersfoortsche Courant* testifies: "*The New York Herald* receives with 'commercial cable' a story from Chicago that has a remarkable resemblance to an 'April fool's joke.'

"Great excitement reigns at Chicago, according to the account, about the appearance of lights that move fast across the skies. Generally it is believed that it concerns an airship, which has been talked about for weeks now.

"Astronomers though claim that those lights are nothing else but stars. Professor Hough of the Northwestern University says, that after a careful investigation he has come to the conviction that the light originates from the star Alpha Orionis. The airship, or the star, was discovered Friday evening at about nine o'clock, moving towards the northeast and apparently 1,000 feet above the ground. The light moved very fast; it was followed by a number of smaller lights.

"Mr. Harmar, secretary of the Aeronautical Society in Chicago, claims that the lights in fact originate from an airship with three persons on board, of whom he knows one.

"The ship is made of paper and left San Francisco several weeks ago. Professor Octave Chanute and several rich persons are involved with the undertaking and provided the necessary money.

"A telegram from Topeka, Kansas, says that the same light was seen there on March 27; some have seen a fireball, others maintain that they truly saw an airship.

"In Belleville it is claimed that the same light was seen there on March 16 for three quarters of an hour, after which it quickly disappeared. On the evening of March 27 an immense crowd waited for the advent of the light, which showed itself again, this time at ten o'clock. This time it was so strong that it illuminated the windowpanes. Hundreds, including the Governor, saw the light appear over Topeka."(21)

Thanks to digital archives, we can follow the progression of the accounts through the newspapers even on an international scale and can see how, when reported in local newspapers far removed from the original events, they can now give a context for the reporting of local anomalous events, as we have seen in the case of the Flying Man of Coney Island, for instance. There is also the timescale to be considered; while Loren Coleman has commented on how quickly television and the internet disseminated the Chupacabra phenomenon(22), we can also note, as Coleman does, that the time periods over which specific anomalies were disseminated through the 19th century newspapers were much longer, which provided different timescales for the gestation of these anomalies in 19th century popular culture. There is also the international aspect with regard to the 19th and early 20th century references of fortean phenomena that sheds light on the various cultural differences and the various ways in which coverage took place: from the sober to the credulous; from the matter-of-fact to joking, skeptical, or sarcastic editorial viewpoints, undoubtedly reflecting some of the cultural climate of a place or community. And sometimes we may even find new, but similar, anomalous events of a local nature mixed in and described in the newspapers.

The Thing from the Magnus Quarry

While I may sound very optimistic in terms of the newspaper digitization process – and I honestly think that it will come to revolutionize the fields of fortean research one day – the analog hunting methods, which involve having to slowly and painstakingly wade through the physical newspaper pages themselves or scanning reels of microfilm, is still an absolute necessity that definitely cannot be abandoned at this stage. After all, just a fraction of the newspapers that once existed are digitized, and then not all newspapers have been preserved. Some are still only found in a state, regional, or city archive or library, in a newspaper morgue somewhere in an ill lit basement, or as incomplete runs that are lovingly preserved by the many historical societies that are found in almost every state in America. Discoveries of a previously unknown fortean gem found the old way still occur frequently, where digital research is the complementary instrument. Canadian fortean researcher Ritchie Benedict found the item below through diligently scanning newspapers in the Canadian newspaper archives, the contents of which have not been digitized. Since his extremely interesting find is not mentioned in the fortean literature, I conducted a search for this account in the digital archives and was able to trace a fragment of its history through various American newspapers.

The Canadian newspaper *Daily Sun* reported in its October 23, 1893 edition: "As Mrs. Caspar Mann and Mrs. Joseph Godwick, two well-known ladies of that section, were returning home in a buggy about sunset, they heard an unnatural noise in passing along the road south of the Magnus quarry. The noise was a cross between a bellow and a shriek and excited the curiosity of the hearers, but as they could not locate it but little attention was paid to it, and they continued on their journey. In approaching a lonely spot on the road where large forest trees stand on both sides and the ground along is covered with underbrush they heard the awful noise again. This time it appeared to come from the boughs of a large tree just ahead of them. As they approached the tree there was a commotion in the branches, and the lonely and helpless women were horrified to see a horrible-looking monster descending from the tree coon-fashion. Their horse seemed paralyzed with fear, and for a moment refused to answer the frantic effort of the driver to force him ahead.

"As the animal reached the ground it gave a terrific snort and roar and started for the buggy. One of the occupants seized the whip and prepared for the attack. Recovering his sense of locomotion the horse started at a brisk gait down the road. Then the race for life began. The strange monster, although peculiarly constructed, made excellent time, and in a few minutes had overtaken the buggy and was making frantic efforts to climb up on the box in the rear. The lady with the whip laid on the lash with all her might in the hope of frightening the fearful looking animal off, but the stings of the whip only seemed to infuriate it and increase its determination to devour everything in sight.

"As the women were about to give up the fight and surrender themselves to the rapacious brute the joyful sound of the bark of a friendly dog fell upon their ears, and they realized they were nearing a farm-house. To their gratification two men stepped out in the road a short distance in front of them, and it was but the work of a moment for the women to notify them of their terrible predicament. As the men and dogs approached, the animal seemed to sniff danger, and, with a roar that could be heard for a quarter of a mile, whirled to one side and ambled through the brush, its course could be plainly discerned by the waving branches.

"The men, being unarmed, did not deem it wise to follow the animal, and the dogs showed no disposition to take up the chase.

"More dead than alive, the women were assisted into the farm-house, where they were given such stimulants as were at hand, and when sufficiently recovered they related their experience as given above.

"The animal, they say, was about seven feet long. Its head was long, and ended in a beak like an eagle's; it's body was round, like that of an alligator, covered with scales and ornamented with a pair of wings, which would probably measure six feet from tip to tip.

"It had four legs, and its feet were cloven and covered with a hoof. The smell of its breath and body was terrible, and pervaded the atmosphere for some time after it had escaped to its retreat in the woods. In its effort to climb unto the buggy the animal left unmistakable proof of its hoofs on the buggy-bed, there being deep cuts and scratches all over the rear of the vehicle.

"The spot where the animal made its appearance and the country for miles around is lonely and seldom frequented by farmers or others, and is certainly just the place for a wild animal of any kind to seek its lair.

"Inquiry of scientists and naturalists fails to throw any light on the existence anywhere of such an animal as this, and it is probable a searching party will be organized in the hope of capturing it, and thus adding another curiosity to zoology – *Greensburg cor. Cininnati Enquirer.*"(23)

I located the account in four American newspapers: from Illinois, Indiana, Louisiana, and Wisconsin. (24) It was published in these newspapers in abbreviated form, between September 25 and October 12, 1893, so far making the Canadian newspaper account the last one and also the longest one. For purposes of comparison, I cite an example of its abbreviated format as it was published in an Illinois newspaper, the *Decatur Daily Republican*: "Greensburg, Ind. Sept. 24 – Mrs. Caspar Mann and Mrs. Jos Groswick were returning home in a buggy, Friday evening when they heard an unusual noise from the woods along the road. A moment later a horrible creature descended a tree coon-fashion, and running after the buggy tempted to climb up behind. There was a race for life that continued a mile when two men with dogs were met and the monster fled into the woods. The animal was seven feet long. Its head ended in a beak like an eagle's its body was round like that of an alligator, covered with scales and ornamented with a pair of wings."

The headers of the four American newspapers show something of the spectrum of editorial approach; the Illinois newspaper suggested in its header that the creature had probably escaped from "a Chinese Bazaar;" the Indiana newspaper called the creature a "varmint," harking back to the varmint tradition in cryptozoology; the Louisiana newspaper called it "The biggest snake story," clearly expressing its opinion as to the improbability of the tale by referring to the yearly returning crop of weird and wonderful tales of immense snakes, hoop snakes, and all kinds of larger-than-life, von Munchausen-like yarns involving serpents. The Wisconsin newspaper called the creature a "boojum." It cited the *Indianapolis Journal*, and while I have not found the account as this newspaper has not been digitized, it indicates that the story had a broader and nationwide exposure, stretching beyond what I was able to locate and retrieve. So far I have not found it in an Indiana newspaper – at least, the digitized ones currently available to us in the online archives – and we have no indication of a specific date for the incident, only having the dates of the first publications as an indicator. As to the event itself, there is every reason to speculate that, as soon as the local Greensburg newspapers are located, we might find nothing referring to the incident or the account of an entirely different incident involving the same persons.

As an example of this I'll quote a case that I researched and have included in my paper on Spring-heeled Jack in America that will be published under the editorship of former publisher of *Fortean Times* and Spring-heeled Jack expert Mike Dash. Citing the accounts that I found in the digital archives, I first treated the Delaware Devil in my appendix on the Black Flash of Cape Cod that was published in *Anomalist 13*.(25) It is a haunting scare that involved a seven foot black phantom that terrorized the inhabitants of Georgetown, Delaware, in 1909, according to what some newspapers of that time reported. My research into the Delaware Devil case proved to me the benefits of analog and digital research combined as an ideal approach when trying to get to the bottom of this story. Occasionally, I publish a blog on the website of the Charles Fort Institute, and I was first made aware of the case there, thanks to a blog entry by Mike Dash.(26)

The Strange Case of the Delaware Devil

The deeper we travel into the epicenter of the bizarre occurrences in Georgetown, Delaware, the more the story diverges from the story as reported by newspapers further away. For this reason we will approach the strange case of the Delaware Devil as reported in the newspapers in reverse chronological order. A single, fascinating account was published late April and early May in two out-of-state newspapers, one from the District of Columbia, the other from Texas. The account told of a weird creature terrorizing parts of Georgetown: "Georgetown, Del. April 28. – More than seven feet in height and swathed in a long black cloak, closely wrapped around its face, a new mystery has been exciting some parts of Georgetown, where it has followed women and young girls and jumped out from behind trees at them. The 'Devil in Black,' as it is called, first appeared several nights ago, when a dozen or so persons saw it during the course of the evening. From behind a tree it jumped at Mrs. William Curdy and sent her screaming with fright into a neighbor's house, while a daughter of Joseph Carnel also was chased by the mysterious stranger until she fell almost fainting into Fred Rust's grocery store. The men of the neighborhood, informed of the affair, led by William Curdy, ran across fields, jumped fences and through back yards, with the 'Devil' but a few yards ahead of them, but, while crossing the big ditch known as the Savannah, the figure completely disappeared and, despite search, could not be found. Again it was seen by several young girls and last night it made its appearance and was seen closely by Mrs. Carn Josephs, who heard a noise as she passed her woodshed. She turned to look and distinctly saw the 'Devil' walk out of the shed and after her. Almost fainting with fear she ran screaming into the house, while her husband ran into the yard with his gun and fired at the tall figure, which was plainly distinguished at the woodshed. In a second it was gone with no trace of injury from the gun. Many superstitious declare that bullets cannot hit it, but some of the more determined men declare it is the work of a practical joker and expect to put a load of shot into it at their first opportunity."(27)

Despite numerous extensive searches, these two accounts were all that I located in the digitized newspaper archives. I contacted the Delaware Historical Society and upon my request numerous extensive searches were conducted in five Delaware newspapers that have not been digitized and are only accessible as physical objects in situ. The newspapers were the *Every Evening*, *Delawarean*, *Milford Chronicle*, *Sunday Star*, and *Morning News*, a newspaper that was published in

Wilmington, a community in the vicinity of Georgetown.(28) Only the *Morning News* referred to unusual happenings that befell Georgetown during the estimated timeframe of the "Devil in Black" scare. Although no less strange, they are very different from, and perhaps less spectacular than, the out-of-state accounts of the seven foot tall, black-cloaked creature. The first item, published on April 27, reported on strange occurrences in Georgetown the morning two days before, with the highly interesting detail that William Curdy was again involved: "A strange and unaccountable sound was heard early yesterday morning by the residents of Kimmeystown, a suburb of this town, and has caused considerable consternation among the inhabitants. It was first heard about 1 o'clock, and soon many of the families were up making an investigation but nothing could be seen that would clear the mystery. The noise, it is said, sounded like a woman, who was undergoing great pain; and repeatedly the words 'Oh! My God,' were heard by those making the search.

"The first family to hear the strange noise was that of George Walls, who resides at the corner of Cedar street and Albury avenue, and so lamentable did the noise become that the families of John T. Calhoun, William J. Curdy, Wingate Conaway, Levin Derrickson and James A. Carey were aroused. More than a score of persons began to scour the neighborhood looking for the strange omen, but nothing could be found. During the excitement, which prevailed, Mrs. John Calhoun, wife of a well known barber here, became so badly frightened that she fainted and suffered a nervous collapse and medical attention had to be rendered. She is still suffering from the shock. At first it was believed that some woman was being murdered, but a strict search throughout the section and down the ditches and in the woods nearby fails to bring anything of that nature to light. The old inhabitants of the town, who have faith in weird sounds and omens, state that a great calamity is going to befall the town."(29)

Two days later "many of the residents of Kimmeytown were again frightened by the same peculiar sound which was heard the other evening. The strange noise, which it is said sounds like the voice of a woman in agony, was not of long duration last night. Residents of that section are unable to account for it."(30)

Judging from the accounts in the local press, the story of a giant, black-clad phantom springing out of nowhere and terrorizing the neighborhoods of Georgetown obviously originated from somewhere else, perhaps in an editorial office far away, perhaps in the mind of an enterprising journalist. There is comfort in this scenario and one might feel inclined to adopt it as a logical explanation and leave it at that. The inherent symbolism of the data as encapsulated in the black-clad giant imbued with supernatural powers and prowess makes one wonder if such a potent image was purely, merely, and only a fanciful concoction. Many of the 19th and 20th century urban scares involved black-clad entities springing out of nowhere and terrorizing whole communities before disappearing again through that otherworldly looking glass.

If the Delaware Devil was a tale of fiction and we have every reason to believe it is, it clearly harked back to a tradition of black phantoms who terrorized entire neighborhoods, and by touching on this raw nerve buried deep in the fiber of whole communities, it was successful as a tale that was printed in several newspapers and went unchallenged for a century. In the end the Delaware Devil may not have existed, but we must not forget, however, how Georgetown was struck by strange and unexplainable events in the timeframe that the phantom allegedly haunted the community.

The Mohican magnetic anomaly

Often, but not always, does research yield a string of accounts and we remain stuck, no matter how hard we search, with that one puzzling account that tells of an incredibly weird event, but beyond that we can find no other corroborating or perhaps explicatory accounts of the event in question. An example of the nationwide distribution of a Fortean anomaly, of which we have just the one account, is found in the strange incident with the magnetic cloud that befell the ship *Mohican* in 1904. I first read about the incident more than a decade ago. It was located by Michael Shoemaker in the August 1, 1904 issue of the *Philadelphia Inquirer*.(31) Delving in the various digital newspaper archives, I located the account in 21 other American newspapers (32) – one referring to yet another American newspaper where it was published – and one Canadian (33), which indicates that the incident enjoyed more than a nationwide coverage. The case was intriguing enough for John Keel to connect it with the rumors of the ill-fated Philadelphia Experiment (34), and now that we have seen how the tale was widely published throughout America it is not a suggestion that is easily brushed off.

For those not readily familiar with the event, I cite one of the apparently many – but similar – newspaper articles that were published in the month of August 1904: "As the British ship Mohican made for the Delaware breakwater yesterday it encountered a strange phenomenon. A cloud of phosphorous enveloped the vessel, magnetizing everything on board. Capt. Urquhart tells the story and the crew vouch for the details.

"'I noticed a strange gray cloud at a distance, and watched it as it came closer. The vessel and crew were given a fiery coating before the sailors saw it,' said the captain. 'They rushed about the deck in consternation. I looked at the needle and it was flying around like an electric fan. I ordered several of the crew to remove several of the iron chains lying around the deck, thinking it would divert their attention.

"'But the sailors could not budge the chains, although they did not weigh more than seventy-five pounds. Everything was magnetized, and chains, bolts, spikes and bars were as tight to the deck as if they had been riveted. The cloud was so dense it was impossible for the vessel to proceed. I could not see beyond the decks, and it appeared as if the whole world was a mass of glowing fire.

"'The frightened sailors fell on the decks and prayed. The hair on all our heads and beards stuck out like bristles. We noticed that it became difficult to move our arms and legs.

"'Suddenly the cloud began to lift. The phosphorescent glow of the ship and crew began to fade. Gradually the magnetism of the steel died. At the same time the stiffness left our hair. In a few moments the cloud had passed over the vessel and we saw it move off over the sea.

"'I have never encountered a cloud like that. It must have been composed of some magnetized substance which was combined with phosphorous.'"(35)

All the accounts that I located harbor the same details and in general they are remarkably consistent: the same story without any embellishments is published nationwide. The editorial tone runs the usual gamut from the reporting of plain fact to the skeptical or outright sarcastic, as is witnessed by some of the captions and headers that these newspapers carried. "Was There Double Grog? The Queer Happenings that Set a Vessel's Crew in Consternation," the Ohio newspaper *The Mansfield News* asked its readers, or, "New Kind Of Sea Serpent. Captain of the Mohican Says Vessel and Crew Were Enveloped in Phosphoric Vapor," read the caption of Texas newspaper *The Galveston Daily News*. Yet another newspaper from San Antonio, Texas, bluntly presented the story with the caption: "A Munchausen Tale Told By Ship Captain."

It is well to take into account that editorial sarcasm does not necessarily imply that a tale is a hoax or a yarn that is cleverly dismantled by this or that newspaper. Writing about the 1896-1897 airship wave in his *The Great Airship Mystery*, Daniel Cohen remarks on the dubious role of newspaper owners in regards to commenting on stories or accounts published by competing newspapers: it had more to do with territorial rivalry than the need for accurate and honest reporting.(36)

But what about the *Mohican* and her subsequent fate? I found no further follow-ups such as official reports or outcomes of official investigations with regard to Captain Urquhart's strange story. While not an expert on matters and procedures maritime, I would assume that an official report was prepared as well for the company who owned the vessel. I decided to trail the whereabouts of the ship during the month of August in the "News of the Ships and the Shipping men" section of the *Philadelphia Inquirer*. *Mohicans*'s subsequent fate was not quite a merry one. Having set forth on another voyage from Philadelphia for Ibrail, August 22 found the *Mohican* "badly stranded at Kipez Point, Dardanelles." Fortunately, assisting ships were with her. *Mohican*'s cargo was valued at $200,000 consisting of iron piping, boilers, and machinery. A day later she was discharging her cargo, as "salvage steamers having failed to float her." More news on her condition was published a few days later: "*Mohican* on a sandy bottom. Steamer *Mohican* (Br). Urquhart from Philadelphia for Ibrail, which as before reported, went ashore at Kipez Point, in the Dardanelles, is lying broadside to the shore on a sandy bottom. The work of lightening the steamer and dredging to float her is being continued." On August 27, the *Mohican* was floated and arrived at Chanak: "The *Mohican* is not leaking. The reloading of her cargo will probably be completed Monday."(37)

One would be curious to learn what the exact cause was that made the *Mohican* strand at Kipez Point, if, for instance, an erratic, strangely behaving compass needle might have exacted its toll. One wonders if the *Mohican* had become one of those vessels that sailors, who listen to premonitions and intuitions about because their lives depend on it, dread to man. A ship of doom with a mischievous jinx that like Frankenstein's monster was dragged to life by the forces of electricity, waking the *Mohican*, all of its steel hull, its rivets, its joints, its tonnage, its boilers and compartments, and giving it a blind and dumb but remorseless sentience of its own, driving it to a beach somewhere remote. Remote in that the Dardanelles are an intriguing Fortean node; Troy is found in its vicinity, but also Gallipoli, the place where, according to rumors, an entire British regiment vanished without a trace in a mysterious cloud during World War I.(38)

The Crawfordsville Flying Monster

Charles Fort has much to say on interpreting newspaper accounts apart from the almost binary – and therefore very limited – approach of false, not false, true account or yarn, tall tale or hoax.

In his third book, *Lo!*, Fort writes about the weird flying, headless monster that startled the inhabitants of Crawfordsville, Indiana, in September 1891, and again calling the flying anomaly "a construction," while citing the *Brooklyn Daily Eagle* (39), a newspaper that is digitized and accessible online: "Brooklyn Eagle, Sept. 10, 1891 – something that was seen, at Crawfordsville, Indiana, 2 a.m., Sept. 5th. Two icemen saw it. It was a seemingly headless monster, or it was a construction, about 20 feet long, and 8 feet wide, moving in the sky, seemingly propelled by fin-like attachments. It moved toward the icemen. The icemen moved. It sailed away, and made such a noise that the Rev. G.W. Switzer, pastor of the Methodist church, was awakened, and, looking from his window, saw the object circling in the sky.

"I supposed that there was no such person as the Rev. G.W. Switzer. Being convinced that there had probably never been a Rev. G.W. Switzer, of Crawfordsville – and taking for a pseudo-standard that if I'm convinced of something that is something to suspect – I looked him up. I learned that the Rev. G.W. Switzer had lived in Crawfordsville, in September 1891. Then I found out his present address in Michigan. I wrote to him, and received a reply that he was traveling in California, and would send me an account of what he had seen in the sky, immediately after returning home. But I have been unable to get him to send that account. If anybody sees a 'headless monster' in the sky, it is just as well to think that over, before getting into print. Altogether, I think that I make here as creditable and scientific a demonstration as any by any orthodox scientist, so far encountered by us. The problem is: Did a 'headless monster' appear in Crawfordsville, in September 1891? And I publish the results of my researches: 'Yes, a Rev. G.W. Switzer did live in Crawfordsville, at the time.'"(40)

We can add that accounts of the Crawfordsville flying anomaly were published nationwide in a variety of newspapers. Thus far I have located various accounts of different lengths and editorial stances in ten newspapers in various states, again indicating that news on the anomalous, the strange, and the Fortean in the era before Fort traveled through America. (41) Descriptions varied, one Missouri newspaper named the flying anomaly a "monster bird": "Citizens of Indiana need not be alarmed about the monster bird that has been seen hovering over Crawfordsville. It is probably only a large sized cow fattening for Mr. Harrison's consolation dinner in 1892," it commented tongue-in-cheek.

(42) "Is It The Gyasticutus?" a South Carolina newspaper (43) jokingly wondered, slyly referring to the menagerie of other improbable creatures of folklore that nobody took very seriously, although some of these might have had some basis in fact, unbelievables such as the Dwayyo, the Wahoo, the Hodag, or the Glastonbury Glawackus.

Unfortunately, my research on this specific Fortean anomaly yielded no as-yet-unknown accounts of similar events in other places in the same timeframe. We must always bear in mind though that one account in one publication merits the search for other publications in other newspapers, or the approach of research in situ as Jerome Clark demonstrated in his solving of Alexander Hamilton's yarn about alien airship pilots stealing a calf that allegedly had occurred during the great 1896-1897 airship wave (44). Needless to say the diligent unearthing of newspaper accounts and the recovery of similar tales, or the discovery that a story was more widespread than was previously known, is no guarantee for veracity.

The 19th and 20th century newspapers were riddled with hoaxes, but, if anything, they are a fitting testimony to the inventiveness and playful nature of our ancestors. They offer an enchanted glimpse in the way our ancestors enjoyed, played with, wondered about, and pondered our haunted planet and its many denizens. The various versions, the shorter, longer, cynical, condescending, fanciful, humorous, or sober ones help us perceive the larger context in which these Fortean accounts appeared in the pre-Fort era. As such, they form a fascinating topography of the damned. We may eventually even be forced to re-evaluate the pre-Fort fortean mindset of 19th century culture by the sheer weight of new publication data and take a closer look at the existence of a widespread tradition in which these tales flourished and were published time and again. What needs were served and what their function was in our society may be newly debated, especially in the light of a certain tendency of seeking influences in a too one-dimensional mode, as if every obscure 19th century tale of proto-science fiction automatically would have generated accounts of strange lights seen in the skies where there is a multitude of other foundations and sources to be taken into account.

The digital revolution that is underway is only the beginning, and already it has invited us to embark on the journey through the kaleidoscope. What we find on the other side and what we encounter there would have delighted Charles Fort in no small measure.

Notes

1. "Monkeys Seen Near Sedalia," *Daily Capital News*, Jefferson City,

Jefferson, Missouri, August 8, 1959.

2. On the aspect of escapees from traveling circuses or circus train wrecks, see Loren Coleman, *Mysterious America*, Paraview Press, the revised edition, 2001, pages 78-79 and 208.

3. "Tales of the Beaman Monster still linger," *Constitution-Tribune*, Chillicothe, Missouri, February 19, 2008.

4. Charles Fort, *Lo!*, Claude Kendall, 1931, chapter 17, page 207. Also here: www.resologist.net/lo117.htm#N_3_

5. Notes Mr. X on Fort's source: *New York Sun*, April 25, 1885, (Not found here). Fort erred here in that the brief item was published in *The Sun*, Baltimore, Maryland, April 25, 1885. The account was published in various American newspapers; so far I noted publications in the *Daily Index-Appeal*, Petersburg, Virginia, April 27, 1885; *The Landmark*, Statesville, North Carolina, May 1, 1885; *Augusta Chronicle*, Augusta, Georgia, May 27, 1885; and the *Macon Weekly Telegraph*, Macon, Georgia, May 27, 1885. *The Landmark*, May 1, 1885 entry differs somewhat from the accounts above in that it concludes: "...The list of such disappearances in the western portion of Virginia in the past few months is remarkable, quite a number having occurred during that time, and no clue has ever been discovered to any of them." Since Fort mentions this detail that is not found in his listed sources, we may conclude that Fort used other sources for his entries that he not always cared to reference.

6. "His Body Found," *Macon Weekly Telegraph*, Macon, Georgia, May 27, 1885.

7. Loren Coleman, *Mothman and other curious encounters*, Paraview Press, 2002, second edition, page 93.

8. "Wild Man Of The Woods. A Wonderful Prodigy Captured in the Wilds of Tennessee and Brought in Louisville for Exhibition – His Body Covered with Fish Scales," *The Galveston Daily News*, Galveston, Texas, November 2, 1878; *The Herald And Torch Light*, Hagerstown, Maryland, November 13, 1878; "What Is It. The Wild Man of the Woods Captured in the Wilds of Tennessee," *Warren Ledger*, Warren, Pennsylvania, November 15, 1878; "The Wild Man of Tennessee," *Lowell Weekly Sun*, Lowell, Massachusetts, November 23, 1878.

9. "The 'Man-Fish' of Tennessee – A Case of Ichthyosis," *Waterloo Courier*, Waterloo, Iowa, December 25, 1878.

10. Charles Fort, *Lo!*, Claude Kendall, 1931, chapter 12, page 142. For the correct *Zoologist* citation, see: "Lo! A Hypertext Edition of Charles Hoy Fort's Book, Edited and Annotated by Mr. X." note 14, at www.resologist.net/lo112.htm

11. "Este es Cuento," *El Constituyente*, Copiapo, Chile, March 18, 1868. See: Liliana Núñez and Fabio Picasso, "El Caso De La Mina Fantasma – Copiapó, 1868," *Archivos Forteanos Latino Americanos*, 2007, www.aforteanosla.com.ar/afla/articulos%20crypto/copiapo%201868.htm

12. "A New Monster," *Morning Herald*, Titusville, Pennsylvania, May 18,

1868; "A New Monster," *The Janesville Gazette*, Janesville, Wisconsin, May 18, 1868; "A Monster of the Air – A Very Strange Story," *Milwaukee Daily Sentinel*, Milwaukee, Wisconsin, Monday, May 18, 1868; " A New Monster," *Bangor Daily Whig & Courier*, Bangor, Maine, May 19, 1868; " A Monster of the Air – A Very Strange Story," *Memphis Daily Avalanche*, Memphis, Tennessee, May 20, 1868; " A Monster of the Air – A Very Strange Story," *Morning Oregonian*, Portland, Oregon, June 6, 1868; " A Monster of the Air," *The Cheyenne Leader*, Cheyenne, Wyoming, June 12, 1868; " The Fiery Dragon of the Cordilleras," *Frank Leslie's Illustrated Newspaper*, New York, New York, June 13, 1868.

13. " A Monster of the Air – A Very Strange Story," *Milwaukee Daily Sentinel*, Milwaukee, Wisconsin, May 18, 1868.

14. Fort cites an earlier one from 1877, and in the context of his fascination with mechanical aspects of anomalies, it is interesting to note that this sighting, published as a letter the *New York Sun*, involves something of which it is lightheartedly suggested that it might have been an angel. In: Charles Fort, *Lo!*, Claude Kendall, 1931, chapter 12, page 142. See also: " Lo! A Hypertext Edition of Charles Hoy Fort's Book, Edited and Annotated by Mr. X," www.resologist.net/lo112.htm#N_13_ Fort's source: Wm. H. Smith. "Was it an angel?" *New York Sun*, September 21, 1877.

15. "A Flying Machine," *Louisville Courier-Journal*, Louisville, Kentucky, July 29, 1880.

16. "An Aerial Mystery," *The Fitchburg Sentinel*, Fitchburg, Massachusetts, September 14, 1880; "An Aerial Mystery," *The News and Observer*, Raleigh, North Carolina, September 15, 1880; "An Aerial Mystery," *Daily Arkansas Gazette*, Little Rock, Arkansas, September 18, 1880.

17. "Other Viewpoints. Flutter of Dark Wings," *The Abilene Reporter-News*, Abilene, Texas, June 6, 1948.

18. Charles Fort, *The Book of the Damned*, Boni and Liveright, 1919, chapter 21, page 261 (top of page), *The Complete Books of Charles Fort*, Dover edition, 1974, pages 273-274 (bottom and top), hypertext edition here: www.resologist.net/damn21.htm

19. *Texelse Courant*, Texel, the Netherlands, March 11, 1888.

20. *Nieuwe Amersfoortsche Courant*, Amersfoort, the Netherlands, March 24, 1888. We note that again, Fort omits to mention the interesting statement that the captain "had observed such a phenomenon at Cape Race before," a detail that, as in the Copiapó account, throws new light on these phenomena. This opens up a new area of research into what John Keel termed "window areas," certain geographic locales where we witness a cluster of anomalous events over time. Possibly the allusions to repetitions at Copiapo and Cape Race point toward previously uncharted local traditions or a folklore involving anomalous events.

21. "Gemengd Nieuws. Een Aprilgrap?," *Nieuwe Amersfoortsche Courant*, Amersfoort, the Netherlands, April 17, 1897.

22. Loren Coleman, *Mothman and other curious encounters*, Paraview Press,

2002, second edition, page 105.

23. "What Was It? Horrible Monster That Attacked Two Women on a Lonely Road," *Daily Sun*, St. John, New Brunswick, Canada, October 23, 1893.

24. "A Horrible Monster. Probably Escaped from the Chinese Basaar in the Midway Plaisanon," *Decatur Daily Republican*, Illinois, Decatur, September 25, 1893; "Monster Seen Near Greensburg," Two Women Chased by a Nondescript "Varmint," *Logansport Pharos*, Logansport, Indiana, September 25, 1893; "The Biggest Snake Story," *Times Picayune*, Louisiana, New Orleans, September 28, 1893; "Strange Stories By Telegraph. Chased by a Tree-Climbing Boojum," *The Milwaukee Journal*, Milwaukee, Wisconsin, October 12, 1893. Cites the *Indianapolis Journal*.

25. Theo Paijmans, "The Black Flash Of Cape Cod: True Heir Of Spring-heeled Jack," *Intermediate States, Anomalist 13*, eds. Patrick Huyghe and Dennis Stacy, Anomalist Books, 2007, pages 34-35.

26. Mike Dash, "Serendipity And Spring-heeled Jack," http://blogs.forteana.org/node/16, May 24, 2007.

27. "Town Is Terrorized By A 'Devil In Black.' Mysterious Giant Figure Keeps Georgetown, Del., Guessing – Appears at Night Before Women and Children. Superstitious Say It Can't Be Harmed by Bullets," *Washington Times*, Washington, District of Columbia, April 28, 1909; "Town Terrorized By Black Devil. Mysterious Giant Figure Keeps Georgetown, Del., Guessing – Frightens Women and Children," *Fort Worth Star-Telegram*, Fort Worth, Texas, May 9, 1909.

28. Reference Librarian Ed Richi of the Delaware Historical Society, Wilmington, Delaware, stated: "Unfortunately there was nothing at all in the *Every Evening* from April 23rd through May 3rd. This was the largest circulating paper. However it focused on northern Delaware so it is not totally surprising that Georgetown news wouldn't be covered much in it." For the *Delawarean* that was a weekly newspaper, the dates 17 and 24 April were searched, also without results. No mention of Georgetown's ghost scare was found in the pages of the *Milford Chronicle* and the *Sunday Star*. E-mail correspondence, various dates.

29. "Many New Notes From The State. Strange Sounds Near Georgetown. They Were Weird and One Woman Was So Badly Frightened That She is Ill," *Morning News*, Wilmington, Delaware, April 27, 1909.

30. "Frightened by a Noise," *Morning News*, Wilmington, Delaware, April 29, 1909.

31. John Keel, "The Great Phonograph In The Sky," *The Fringes Of Reason, A Whole Earth Catalog*, Harmony Books, 1989, pages 165-166. The account appeared as "Electric Cloud Enveloped Ship – Caused Mohican's Sailors To Become Like Animated Magnets – Compass Was Set A-Spinning And Iron Chains Could Not Be Lifted From the Deck," *Philadelphia Inquirer*, Philadelphia, Pennsylvania, August 1, 1904.

32. "Cloud Of Fire. It Envelops a Vessel and Magnetizes Everything Aboard," *The Daily Northwestern*, Oshkosh, Wisconsin, August 1, 1904 (distributed

by Associated Press); "Phenomenon On Delaware," *Oakland Tribune*, Oakland, California, August 1, 1904; "Steamship Encounters Strange Phenomenon," *The Cedar Rapids Evening Gazette*, Cedar Rapids, Iowa, August 1, 1904; "This Sailor Saw Things. A Captain Says His Ship Was Wrapped in Phosphorescent, Magnetic Cloud," *Kansas City Star*, Kansas City, Missouri, August 1, 1904; "Strange Phenomenon. Cloud of Phosphoric Appearance Enveloped the Vessel," *Ogden Standard Examiner*, Ogden, Utah, August 1, 1904; "Was There Double Grog? The Queer Happenings that Set a Vessel's Crew in Consternation," *The Mansfield News*, Mansfield, Ohio, August 1, 1904; "Phosphoric Cloud Envelops A Ship. It Magnetized Everything on Board and Frightened the Members of the Crew," *Fort Worth Star-Telegram*, Fort Worth, Texas, August 1, 1904; "Ship Enveloped In Magnetic Cloud. Remarkable Experience of Crew of Vessel Off Delaware Breakwater - Men and Boat in Fiery Coating," *Bellingham Herald*, Bellingham, Washington, August 1, 1904; "Strange Phenomenon. Cloud of Phosphoric Appearance Envelops Vessel at Philadelphia," *Daily Kennebec Journal*, Augusta, Maine, August 2, 1904; "Cloud Of Phosphorus Envelops A Vessel," *The Post-Standard*, Syracuse, New York, August 2, 1904; "Encounter Magnetic Cloud. Vessel Enveloped in Fire and Held in Electric Embrace," *Dallas Morning News*, Dallas, Texas, August 2, 1904; "New Kind Of Sea Serpent. Captain of the Mohican Says Vessel and Crew Were Enveloped in Phosphoric Vapor," *The Galveston Daily News*, Galveston, Texas, August 2, 1904; "A Munchausen Tale Told By Ship Captain," *Daily Express*, San Antonio, Texas, August 2, 1904; "Ship In Magnetic Fog. Strange Phosphorescent Vapor Enshrouds The Mohican," *Sun*, Baltimore, Maryland, August 2, 1904; "Magnetic Cloud Enveloped Ship. Phenomenon Brings About Strange State of Affairs on the Mohican," *Boston Journal*, Boston, Massachusetts, August 2, 1904; "Strange Phenomenon Reported," *Springfield Republican*, Springfield, Massachusetts, August 2, 1904; "A Strange Phenomenon – Everything Metallic On Board a Vessel Was Magnetized," *The Bourbon News*, Paris, Kentucky, August 5, 1904; "Steamship Swathed In Metallic Vapor," *Hawaiian Gazette*, Honolulu, Hawaii, August 9, 1904; "Liner Made a Magnet By Phosphoric Cloud. Chains Stick to Deck, needle Rushes Round, and Everything Glows as Though With Fire," *The Washington Times*, Washington DC, August 19, 1904; "A Good One," *The San Francisco Call*, San Francisco, California, August 23, 1904 (cites the *New York Herald* derisively).

33. "Sailors Strange Experience. Ss. Mohican Encounters a Phosphoric Cloud – Entire Vessel Magnetized – Mass Of Glowing Fire," *Manitoba Morning Free Press*, Winnipeg, Manitoba, Canada, August 2, 1904.

34. John Keel, "The Great Phonograph In The Sky," *The Fringes Of Reason, A Whole Earth Catalog*, Harmony Books, 1989, page 165.

35. "Steamship Encounters Strange Phenomenon," *The Cedar Rapids Evening Gazette*, Cedar Rapids, Iowa, August 1, 1904.

36. Daniel Cohen, *The Great Airship Mystery, A UFO Of The 1890's*, Dodd,

Mead & Company, 1981, pages 20-22.

37. "News Of The Ships And The Shipping men," *Philadelphia Inquirer*, Philadelphia, Pennsylvania, August 23, 24, 27, and 28, 1904.
38. For a good overview, see: David Clarke, "The Vanishing Battalion," www. drdavidclarke.co.uk/vanbat.htm
39. Fort's source was "Substitute for the Sea Serpent," *Brooklyn Daily Eagle*, Brooklyn, New York, September 10, 1891.
40. Charles Fort, *Lo!*, Claude Kendall, 1931, chapter 12, pages 141-142. See also: "Lo! A Hypertext Edition of Charles Hoy Fort's Book, Edited and Annotated by Mr. X," www.resologist.net/lo112.htm#N_12_
41. "Monster Of The Air. An Indiana Town Torn Up By A Terrible Sight. Crawfordsville People Think the End of the World is at Hand – A Preacher's Strange Tale," *Davenport Morning Tribune*, Davenport, Iowa, September 8, 1891; "The Great and Awful Day," *Chillicothe Constitution*, Chillicothe, Missouri, September 8, 1891; *Kansas City Times*, Kansas City, Missouri, September 8, 1891; "A Frightful Aerial Monster," *The Salem Daily News*, Salem, Ohio, September 8, 1891; "Is It The Gyasticutus?," *State*, Columbia, South Carolina, September 8, 1891; "Affrighted Hoosiers. Crawfordsville, Ind., People Watching an Aerial Monster with Great Agitation," *Aberdeen Daily News*, Aberdeen, South Dakota, September 8, 1891; "Affrighted Hoosiers. Crawfordsville, Ind., People Watching an Aerial Monster with Great Agitation," *Bismarck Daily Tribune*, Bismarck, North Dakota, September 9, 1891 "Affrighted Hoosiers. Crawfordsville, Ind., People Watching an Aerial Monster with Great Agitation," *Bismarck Tribune*, North Dakota, Bismarck, September 9, 1891 "The Crawfordsville Air Monster," *The Cedar Rapids Evening Gazette*, Iowa, Cedar Rapids, September 11, 1891; *The New Era*, Iowa, Humeston, September 16, 1891.
42. *Kansas City Times*, Kansas City, Missouri, September 8, 1891.
43. "Is It The Gyasticutus?," *State*, Columbia, South Carolina, September 8, 1891.
44. Jerry Clark, *The UFO Encyclopedia: The Phenomenon from the Beginning*, Volume I: A-K, Omnigraphics, 1998, pages 504-505.

Theo Paijmans lives in the Netherlands, where he works as an editor by day and a Fortean researcher by night. He is the author of two books and many articles, published in publications as All Hallows, Strange Attractor, Anomalist, CFZ Yearbooks 2009 *and* 2010, DarkLore *and* Fortean Times. *Theo spoke at the Fortean Times Unconvention 2008, London and the Second Fortean Conference in paris, 2008. He appeared as an expert in a Discovery Channel documentary on the Vril Society.*

EUROPE'S FORGOTTEN VOLCANOES: THE ENIGMA OF OUT-OF-PLACE-VOLCANOES BY ULRICH MAGIN

There are only three countries with volcanoes in Europe: Iceland in the north, and Greece and Italy in the south. Nevertheless, volcanic eruptions have been reported from many other places, sometimes from regions with a volcanic history, but often from mountains that are known to be of sedimentary rock.

I assume the problem of out-of-place volcanoes is a relatively unknown one, so I hereby submit several examples. As far as orthodox science is concerned, while volcanoes may come into existence relatively quickly, even within a few days, they are more or less a permanent feature of the landscape and seldom simply disappear without a trace—at the very least they usually leave lava that can be dated. Also, while catastrophism and creationism often try to challenge conventional geological thinking, I have yet to come across a reference to volcanoes that appear and disappear overnight, leaving not lava flows, but sediments.

These approximately twenty-five instances are exploratory notes toward documenting this otherwise virtually unknown phenomenon.

Norway

Fort collected reports on OOP-volcanoes, although he doesn't mention them in his books as a phenomenon in its own right. But in his notes, there are at least three instances of this curious phenomenon: for 4 and 5 July 1811, he assembled notes on a "doubtful" eruption in northern Norway. (*Pursuit* 71, 1985, p. 114)

Ireland

Ignatius Donnelly, in *Atlantis: the Antediluvian World*, assembled reports about volcanoes around the Atlantic to show the fragility of its shores—in a way, marking the mid-Atlantic ridge long before Alfred Wegener's discovery of continental drift. Science knew little about why volcanoes existed at all, and Donnelly, in chapter iv of his book, not only reported eruptions of real volcanoes but of some imaginary ones as well.

Regarding Ireland, he writes: "Ireland also lies near the axis of this great volcanic area, reaching from the Canaries to Iceland, and it has been many times in the past the seat of disturbance. The ancient annals contain numerous accounts of eruptions, preceded by volcanic action. In 1490, at the Ox Mountains, Sligo, one occurred by which one hundred persons and numbers of cattle were destroyed; and a volcanic eruption in May, 1788, on the hill of Knocklade, Antrim, poured a stream of lava sixty yards wide for thirty-nine hours, and destroyed the village of Ballyowen and all the inhabitants, save a man and his wife and two children. (Ignatius Donelly, *Atlantis: the Antediluvian World.* Forgotten Books 2007, original edition 1882, pp. 37-38) Needless to say, there is no recent volcanism in Ireland, and there was none in the times mentioned by Donnelly.

Scotland

In his famous Carta Marina of 1539, the first map of northern Europe, Olaus Magnus shows an erupting mountain in Caithness, at the northern tip of Scotland, and his accompanying text says: "In Scotland I find many horrible fire holes, in which (like in those of Iceland) sulpher burns, and quite often people and animals fall into them." There are no volcanoes in Caithness (Olaus Magnus: *Die Wunder des Nordens.* Frankfurt: Eichborn 2006, p. 73-text, p. 75-illustration).

The second Scottish example is the first I came across, more than twenty years ago, while I searched local British newspapers for appearances of the Loch Ness monster and sea serpents—my main interest then, so I did not write voluminous notes on other fortean topics other than just note paper and date.

On August 15, 1934, the *Northern Chronicle* of Inverness (p. 4 and 5) carried reports about a volcano that suddenly had erupted on Raasay, in the Hebrides. I remember that several other papers also printed eyewitness reports of the eruption, among them, I believe, *The Inverness Courier* and the London *Times.* Searching the *Scotsman* archives, I found the paper carried a story headlined "Volcanic Manifestations on Isle of Raasay," bylined 27 June 1934 (*Scotsman*, 29 June 1934, p. 13). If I remember the *Northern Chronicle* news story correctly, witnesses observed a full-blown eruption, with lava flows and a cloud of smoke hanging over the crater. Perhaps related to these events (the "eruptions" must have lasted from the end of June to mid-August) is the fact that earthquake tremors were also reported from Raasay and the neighboring island of Skye by the *Scotsman* in mid-August (*Scotsman*, 18 August

1934, p. 9). Although Raasay's highest point, Dun Caan, is an extinct volcano, it has not been active for several million years.

Wales

The Welsh example comes from the pages of *Fortean Times*. In a letter, Richard Holland quoted an *Annual Register* report of 1773 on the eruption of Moel Fammau in Clwyd. As with the other examples, Holland notes: "There are no fragments of lava, ancient or otherwise, anywhere in the vicinity."

The report of 2 February 1773 says: "The night before last, Moel-famma ... was heard to utter, as it were, deep groans; the adjacent hills trembled from their roots. The noise at eleven o'clock was like the sound of a distant thunder ... At twelve there was a loud clap, and the vortex of the hill threw up in the same instance vast bodies of combustible matter; liquid fire rolled amongst the heaps of ruins; at the close of all, nature seemed to make a grand effort, and rent one side of the mountain, which was solid stone, into an hiatus, whose breadth seemed to be about 200 yards; the summit of the hill tumbled into this vast opening; and the top appears level, which before was almost perpendicular. ... [I]n the places where the fires melted the snow, the earth throws out the verdure of May." (Richard Holland: "Moving Bog and a Welsh Volcano." *Fortean Times* 56, p. 69-70)

The whole thing had been, as Thomas Pennant told novelist Hester Thrale, a simple hoax (Roger Musson: "Moving Bog and Welsh Volcano." *Fortean Times* 57, p. 69)

England

Chris Chatfield's unreferenced webpage on curious natural phenomena, *Cabinet of Curiosities*, relates several instances of volcanoes in England. The first comes from 4 August 1133, when, during an earthquake in England, "Holinshed says also that huge fires burst out of rifts in the earth, and could not be extinguished."

Then, in August 1751, "after hot weather and rain, the cliffs of Charmouth in Dorset began to smoke, then burnt 'with a visible but subtle flame.' The flames were visible at intervals, especially after rain, till winter." (*http://www.phenomena.org.uk/curiosities.htm*)

Peter Christie discovered another example in the *Gentleman's Magazine* of 1758, p. 477 (reprinted in *Fortean Studies* 2, p. 260): on 14 October of that year, "a most astonishing phaenomenon" took place at Great Malvern in Worcester: "It had the appearance of a vulcano." It was "attended with a noise as if 100 forges had been at work at once; it filled the air with a nauseous sulphureous smell; it rose from the mountains in the form of a prodigious thick smoak [*sic*], and proceeded to the valleys, where it rose and fell several times, and at length it subsided in a turnepfield, where the leaves of the turneps, leaves of trees, dirt, stick, &c., filled the air and flew higher than the highest hills. It was preceded with the most dreadful storm of thunder and lightning ever heard in the memory of man, and spread an universal consternation wherever it was seen or heard."

Germany

My first German example is from a woodcut reprinted in a wonderful collection of German broadsheets from the 16th and 17th century. It was done by one Hans Moser of Augsburg and relates something extraordinary that happened in the Rhine plains off the Black Forest:

"I am Abraham Weg, the priest of Ballrechten in the Breisgau, and I report herewith for everybody that I have seen with my own eyes, and together with thousands of other people, a significant prodigy which is still ceaselessly disporting itself each day.

"Not very far (about two bowshots away) from a village by the name of Lipburg which is in the territory of Badenweiler in the Breisgau, half a mile from Neuenburg at the Rhine, and half way up a mountain, there is a mountain called Reyenberg or Pflug, and it is connected to the Blauen. There, on the Sunday of Letare in lent, on March 9, 1562, roaring and horrible knocking was heard, and a mountain opened. And it is a fact that it was seen burning.

"Close by was a plain area with meadows, greens, and fields—beautiful to behold—and with a few trees, all in all some two or three hundred acres. There, the mountains started leaning against each other, and the noise and thunder, sounds like shots or collapsing walls, are still going on and without ceasing.

"Now at the site where no tree grew before, there are many, as if they were planted by design. They stand erect, and none of them falls down. Even as rocks fall on them, these rocks pass between the trees. And it sounds as if they fell into an abyss. In addition, the fire was very tall, higher than a spire, at some places high as a house or a little less. It also spreads toward the front, and does so with a kind of explosion and it flames high at the same time. It is beautiful to behold, green, blue, white, red, and other colors. And it has been burning for the last eight days and is approaching the village. The people have torn down their homes and sheds and they are on the run from the mountain. And the beautiful plain area is now a desert and waste land, nobody may walk there, neither animal nor man. And nobody knows where one is safe or when the fire will extinguish or what God Almighty wants to tell us with it. Also one has to fear that in the case it spreads wider once it gets air, the fire will do much harm with the power that is behind it, as a trustworthy eyewitness has himself been able to observe.

"Also, on this Sunday, Judica, more than a thousand people have waited here until it was night. And the fire has reached the village. The almighty, mild and forgiving God may send his holy and good Spirit in order that we receive his godly warning with pious hearts. To better our lives and to honour his godly name." (Nicoline Hortzitz: *Von den unmenschlichen Taten des Totengräbers Heinrich Krahle zu Frankenstein und andere wahrhaftige "Neue Zeitungen" aus der Frühzeit der Sensationspresse*. Frankfurt; Gatza bei Eichborn 1997, p. 25-26)

Although Breisgau, the land around Freiburg at the border of the Black Forest, is metamorphic in nature, and the Kaiserstuhl, a large extinct tertiary volcano last active fifteen million years ago, looms nearby, no recent volcanic activity is known, and I suppose the upper Rhine plain, which has thousands of micro earth tremors each year, is well monitored by geologists. Also, there are no remains of a young but extinct volcano to be seen at Badenweiler.

However, Badenweiler lies at the margin of the Upper Rhine Graben, a rift valley, and is well known for its geothermal activity since Roman times, when the village was called Aquae Villae and the thermal springs of the region were already used for their baths. Was the Badenweiler volcano a mud volcano, exaggerated by known reports of the eruptions of Mt. Vesuvius? Experts on broadsheets assume that this highly dubious Freiburg volcano was probably an invention based on a description of an eruption of Mt. Vesuvius from another broadsheet.

There are several more instances from Germany, although hardly as clear cut. The Roman historian Tacitus reported a case of "flames shooting up from the ground" in his *Annals* (13, 57) for 58 AD:

"The region of the Ubians who are our allies was struck by an unforeseeable disaster. Fires breaking forth from the ground burned villas, fields, and villages and even spread to the walls of the recently founded colony [Cologne]. It could not be put out, not when rain fell not by river water or any other moisture. Then some of the tribesmen, for a lack of other means and angry about the losses, threw stones from a distance, then, when the flames were less intense, approached and tried to frighten them off like wild animals by beating them with sticks, at last they pulled off their clothes and heaped them on the flames to diminish them."

Cologne is close to Germany's largest coal deposits, but also near the Eifel Mountains, which are the remnants of gigantic volcanic activity that ceased only some ten thousand years ago. In this mountain range, there are still some one hundred and fifty ancient volcano craters, last active about thirty thousand to ten thousand years ago. The earth, though, is not yet quiet, and one can see so-called cold-water geysers that are only secondary volcanic (mineral water is heavily under pressure and erupts when it is bored into). At Andernach, the Namedyer Sprudel or Andernach Geyser erupts once every hundred minutes and spouts water well over 200 ft high. It was discovered in 1903, and was then derelict after a new road was constructed, but it has been restored and will be opened to the public again in 2009 (*Kosmos* 1911, p. 349), and at the so-called Brubbel in Wallenborn, every thirty minutes, a fountain some 4 m (13 ft) high and wide is ejected—a fantastic spectacle. In the caldera of Maria Laach, a large lake-filled crater, visitors can still observe gas bubbles rising in the water.

Less credible, unless what we have is an instance of burning subsurface coal deposits, is an eruption from 937 AD, in Saxony, when a "mountain vomited forth flames in many places." (*http://www.phenomena.org.uk/curiosities.htm*)

What must surely be the most exotic out-of-place-volcano is the artificial creation in the park of Wörlitz Castle near Dessau, now an UNESCO world heritage site. The volcano, a hollow cone on the rocky island Stein in an artificial lake in Wörlitz Park, was built between 1788 and 1794 on the order of Duke Leopold Friedrich Franz of Anhalt-Dessau after the nobleman had seen and climbed Vesuvius on his great Italian tour in 1766, while accompanied by Sir William Hamilton (of Emma Hamilton fame). The architect, Friedrich Wilhelm von Erdmannsdorff, constructed the 17 m (60 ft) mountain of brick and natural rock. The island Stein was to give an idea of Naples, and we find the artificial ruins of an amphitheater on it, as well as a classic style Italian villa built for Hamilton. The volcano was fired with fireworks but fell into disuse and was declared unsafe in 1983. It was restored, and the volcano erupted once more for the first time after two hundred years on 1 September 2005. There are even books on this fascinating piece of garden architecture (MDR 7 September 2005; Kulturstiftung Dessau (ed.): *Der Vulkan im Wörlitzer Park*. Berlin: Nicolai 2005). It has little to do with the geological enigmas discussed here, but shows the fascination of volcanoes, and the wish to have one close, in the time when about half of the cases presented in this paper were reported. We will find similar artificial volcanoes from France and Italy.

France

In the second half of July 1751, rumors spread from the Chamouny Valley northwest of Servoz, now in France (Chamonix) but back then part of the Kingdom of Sardinia, that a volcano had erupted there. The king of Sardinia sent Turin scientist Vitaliano Donati to investigate. In a letter to a friend, he reported:

"Although I was quite doubtful regarding the reality of the alleged new volcano, I hastened to observe this unusual phenomenon with great joy. After I had restlessly hiked for four days and two nights from the Aosta Valley, I was confronted with a mountain which was completely enveloped in smoke, and from which by day and night large masses of rock broke off with a rumbling like thunder or a battery of canon fire, yet far louder. The locals had all moved away from the neighborhood and didn't dare watch the spectacle but from a distance of two miles or more. The complete area was covered with ash-like dust, and in part this dust was spread by the wind to a distance of five [Italian?] miles. All people confirmed that from time to time they had seen smoke which was red at day, and accompanied by flames at night. This all made everyone believe that there was no doubt that a volcano had opened. I analysed the alleged ash and found it to be nothing more than several species of rock smashed to dust; I carefully observed the smoke and saw no flames; I didn't smell sulpher; the streams and springs did not show any trace of sulphorous material. When I had convinced myself that this was not a burning solfatara, I entered the smoke and went alone to the abyss. There I saw a large rock tumble into it, and found that the smoke was nothing but the dust the fall of the rock created. My search soon uncovered the origin of the rockslide. A large portion of the mountain below the part that was collapsing did not consist of layers, but an irregular mass of stone and ground; one could see that there must have been previous rockslides on this mountain which were followed by the large mass of rock in the present year, as it no longer had any support and was hanging over. This mass of rocks consisted of horizontal layers, of which the two lower ones were slate which was extremely fragile, above that were two layers of marble similar to that of Porto-venere, but crossed by transversal clefts. The fifth layer completely consisted of slate with a vertical and completely separated layering, and this layer was on top of the fallen mountain. On the high plateau of the mountain were three lakes, and the water of these leaked continuously into the clefts of the rock, made it loose and destroyed its base. The snow which this year had fallen in larger masses than anybody could remember in Savoy had magnified this effect, and all these waters combined created the fall of three million cubic toises of rock, a mass which formed a large mountain in itself." (Dr. G. H. Otto Volger: *Untersuchungen über das Phänomen der Erdbeben in der Schweiz.* Gotha: Justus Perthes 1857, p. 147-148)

What may be a similar event, from the same general region, or a garbled version of it, was reported on Chris Chatfield's homepage on mysterious natural events for January 1761: "Some days after an earthquake near Grenoble in France, during a terrible storm, the earth opened and flames came out." (*http://www.phenomena.org.uk/curiosities.htm*)

And farther in the west, in France's Central Massif, villagers near Brioude, Haute-Loire, were afraid in March 1985 that the extinct volcanoes around them had reawakened—all because two cows were killed by lightning, and a third was thrown around its stable. At the same moment, all telephones of the village rang and five cows were shaken by an electrical charge. "With a certain unease, they look at the Popie, the Boullergue and the Montgivroux, the three ancient volcanoes which might not be dormant, after all," as the newspaper *Republicain Lorrain* reported on 13 March 1985 (reprinted in *CENAP-Report* 111, May 1985, p. 24). I have been unable to identify the last eruptions of these three volcanoes, but the last eruptions from the region, the Auvergne, were of the volcanoes Pavin, Montcineyre, Estivadoux, and Puy de Montchal, carbon-dated to between 5800 and 6300 BP (Etienne Juvigné and Etienne Gilot: "Alter und Verbreitung der Thephren von Montcineyre- und Pavin-Vulkanen (Zentral Massiv, Frankreich)." *Zeitschrift der Deutschen Gesellschaft für Geowissenschaften*, vol. 137, p. 613-623, 1986).

A different kind of volcano was planned in 1899 for the Paris Exhibition of 1900. Like the one in Wörlitz, it was to be artificial. Designed by M. Sordice, this model of Mt. Vesuvius was planned to be 110 yards high and 165 yards in circumference. "It will be built of iron and steel covered with a surface of vegetable earth and turf, the peak and other rocky parts being rendered in cement." Different routes and a cable lift were to lead up to the summit, and also planned were cinemas on the slopes and refreshment areas. "The crater itself will be strictly modeled on the original, and is so arranged that it will emit smoke throughout the day, three eruptions taking place at fixed hours during the evening, when real molten lava can be seen flowing into specially prepared metal channels." In the interior, visitors would see scenic representations of Dante's Inferno! (*New York Times,* 2 March 1899, quoting the London *Pall Mall Gazette*) What became of this projected extravaganza I do not know, I have not seen any reference to it in reports of the actual exhibition.

Bohemia

In December 1732, says Chris Chatfield's homepage, "flames broke out at openings in the mountains" near Prague. In January 1733, the "burning mountains" were said to "continue to flame out in a terrible manner." (*http://www.phenomena.org.uk/curiosities.htm*)

Switzerland

There is little information, and then only unreferenced, on an alleged eruption in Switzerland, in about August 1738: "A mountain in Fribourgh, Switzerland, was said to have emulated Vesuvius by opening with a terrible noise and casting out fire and stones. A later report said it was merely a forest fire burning for several weeks after a hot summer" (*http://www.phenomena.org.uk/curiosities.htm*). Whether this refers to Freiburg, Germany, volcano of 1562, is difficult to say. Perhaps it is a case in its own right.

On 16 April 1819, Zurich's *Züricher Freytagszeitung* reported that "at the very time when violent tremors shook Palermo in Sicily, a small, fire spouting crater formed near Morbio-Inferiore in canton Ticino [near Chiasso]." Only to correct itself three weeks later, in the 7 May issue: "The fire spouting mountain in the canton Ticino has transformed into a harmless landslide." (Volger, op. cit., S. 265)

While the whole region is active tectonically, there has been no recent volcanism—and no trace of a very recent crater at Chiasso. As it appears, a landslide was interpreted, or misrepresented, as an eruption. (1)

Italy

Just across the border from the Chiasso "crater," at the eastern banks of Lake Como, a real semi-volcanic phenomenon, the so-called mud volcanoes, started in the summer of 2004. These mud volcanoes are the result of pressure on water deep below the surface due to Alpine faulting. The Italian newspaper *La Provincia* of Lecco first mentioned "the eruption of a tiny vulcano" on 11 August 2004 (p. 1 & 23). The "vulcanellos" disrupted a pipeline and destroyed the tarmac of a road at Taceno, just east of Lake Como. Marisa Fondra, a hydrogeologist of the University della Terra of Pavia, speculated the phenomenon was due to mud and mineral water being ejected from a fault in the depths of the earth. The region is tectonically active, with several minor quakes a year. "Vulcanello," the word the geologists used, usually means a tiny mud volcano, such as can be found on the Liparian Islands off the northern coast of Sicily (Vulcano, Stromboli, Lipari, and others). The phenomenon continued for several years, and the mud vulcanoes were still causing problems to the commune of Taceno in 2007 (*La Provincia di Lecco*, 18 April 2007, p. 20). On 18 December 2007 (p. 28), the *Provincia di Lecco* reported that there had been damage to the amount of 50,000 Euros since the summer of 2004!

To the east of Lake Como are the Dolomites, a mountain range of the Alps where erosion has created magnificent rock needles of limestone. In a 1980 potboiler on strange phenomena *Jenseits des Wunderbaren* (Augsburg: Weltbild 1980), there was the story of a small mountain lake in the Dolomites over which, at the finest of weather, a vortex formed which sucked up all the water. Most likely the origin of the story lay in a kaarst phenomenon, when a sinkhole swallows a lake, but it was explained (in the discussion board of the German *Forum.Grenzwissenhomepage*, as the result of a "volcano which is in the lake." In this way, a garbled account of some natural event (which I was unable to verify) was transformed into another out-of-place volcano! (*forum.grenzwissen. de/showthread.php?t=2785*) Though hardly in league with the other accounts discussed here, it may sooner or later surface as a "true story."

The eastern coast of Lake Garda, Italy's largest lake and just south of the Dolomites, consists almost entirely of the massive Monte Baldo. The region is seismic, and when in August 1866, severe quakes shook the region, some newspapers depicted the peaceful mountain "covered in flames" and described it as an erupting volcano. Whether anybody ever reported having seen it break out in 1866 is not recorded, and it appears this eruption was a press invention (Tullio Ferro: *Il lago si racconta. Georgrafie e storie del Garda*. Mantova: Editoriale Sometti 2005, p. 31, 59). Monte Baldo consists of sediments, mainly dolomite formed 210 to fifty million years ago, but due to its seismicity, geothermal springs are known from the bottom of Lake Garda, and there is even a hot thermal lake just west of Lake Garda near Lazise.

Further south in Italy we find real volcanic activity, with mud volcanoes, sulphur fields and Mt. Vesuvius, so any report about eruptions cannot be definitely be defined as out-of-place.

Therefore, two eruptions Julius Obsequens lists in his book of prodigies may be real volcanoes—at least, they happened at real volcanoes, although these are regarded as dormant. For 113 BC, Obsequens (ch. 38) notes that Mount Albanus fumed at night. Geologists think that the last eruption of Mt. Albanus was quite recently, around 1100 BC. Lake Bolsena fills a large volcano crater, and this was created by a large eruption about 370,000 years ago. Some believe it was active as late as 104 BC, namely because of a prodigy recorded by Julius Obsequens (ch. 43) who writes that in this year, at Bolsena, flames issued from the ground.

On non-volcanic Sardinia, Italian head of state Silvio Berlusconi had an artificial volcano built in the gardens of his villa at the Costa Smeralda to entertain guests on the 15 August holiday (*The Independent,* 18 August 2006).

Spain

Charles Fort had several notes for 18 March 1817 on an intense darkness, rain, and quakes in Spain, and a "pumic volcano" "reported to be in "the Sierra de Causeros" (*Pursuit* 72, p. 192). I have been unable to trace any mountain range in Spain by that name, maybe it was a misprint, perhaps Fort copied the name incorrectly. There are no known active volcanoes on the Iberian Peninsula.

Poland

In the 11th century, in his *Gesta Hammaburgensis Ecclesiae Pontificum* Adam of Bremen describes the Slav city of Jumne (modern Wolin in Poland) that later became the fabulously rich but sunken city of Vineta of folklore, the "Atlantis of the Baltic." Adam mentions "a volcano pit which the inhabitants call the Greek fire, and Solinus mentions it, too." Preben Hansson (*Und sie waren doch da.* Bayreuth: Hestia 1990, p. 214) believes this was a nuclear power plant of ancient astronauts, but Ingrid and P. Werner Lange (*Vineta—Atlantis des Nordens.* Leipzig 1988, p. 28, 140-141) and Klaus Goldmann & Günter Wermusch (*Vineta.* Bastei Lübbe: Bergisch Gladbach 1999, p. 83-83) point out this was most likely a signal fire for ships on the Baltic. Actually, Wolin's excavator Wladislaw Filipowiak found a large amount of burnt coal on a hill in a strategic position southwest of the town. Gaius Julius Solinus, a Latin writer of the 3rd century, cannot have been in Jumne, and Greek Fire was only invented in the 7th century, but Solinus left us descriptions of signal fires that were found at many harbors of the Mediterranean.

Russia

"In Moscow the mountain Jeniscey, and three others [are volcanoes]," the 17th century encyclopaedist Zedler reports (vol. 50, col. 353). There are no volcanoes near Moscow today, but perhaps Zedler meant the Russian Empire. 18th century renderings of place-names, especially if from foreign languages, are not easy to decipher. If Zedler meant the river Jennisej in Siberia, his report might refer to authentic and real volcanoes after all.

Romania
For 1838, Charles Fort, in his notes, mentions "q[uake] and flames from earth," an "incipient volcano," in Transylvania (*Pursuit* 67, p. 143).

Greece
There are three active and one dormant volcanoes in Greece today:
• the Methana Peninsula in the eastern Peloponnese where the last eruption was about 1700 at an undersea crater off the northwest coast (discovered 1987), and about 230 BC at the volcano of Kameni Chora, reported by Pausanias (II,34,1) who wrote about flames issuing from the earth, Strabo, and Ovid (*Metamorphoses*. XV, 296-306) describes a new mountain rising from a flat field at Troizen.
• Milos Island, which is dormant. The only recent activity is the eruption of hot gases, so called fumaroles, at Kalamos.
• Nisyros Island off the western coast of Turkey, which last erupted in 1500, and in 1881-1887.
• Santorin whose last eruptions are recorded from 197 BC (when it created a new island), 46/47, 726, 1570-73, 1707-11, 1866-70, 1925-28, 1939-41, and 1950.
However, there are also persistent classical sources claiming the island of Lemnos was a volcano, although there is no geological evidence of any recent volcanism. This out-of-place-volcano is certainly the most witnessed of all nonexistent fire-spouting mountains! Yet, check any of the tourist or hotel websites of Lemnos, and you will read that, until about two thousand years ago, this island in the North Aegean Sea was a volcano. And indeed, many—although not all—classical authors report a "volcanic mountain" or "earth fire" located at a mount later called Mosychlos. Until the early 19th century, it was generally assumed that Lemnos had had a volcano. I stumbled upon this in ancient astronaut author Robert Charroux' *Unbekannt Geheimnisvoll Phantastisch* (Düsseldorf: Econ 1997, p. 137).
The "Lemnian Fire" was first reported by Eustathius and Heraklides Ponticus. Sophocles, in his *Philoktet* (799-801, 814) refers to "the

burning flames rising on Lemnos," while Herodotus (7, 6) knows a fake prophecy that the island will one day be destroyed. But, while Homer calls Lemnos Hephaistos' island in both the Iliad and the Odyssey, the bard knows of no volcano, and similarly ignorant are Thykidides and Appolonios of Rhodes, although all these authors describe the island in great detail.

Mosychlos, the name of the volcanic mountain, is first mentioned by Antimachus (ca. 400 BC) and Eratosthenes (276 BC). Among the Roman writers, several refer to the Lemnos volcano, mainly Varro, Seneca, Valerius Flaccus (in his *Argonautica* bk 1,78, bk 2, 332-336), and Statius (*Theb V,* 49-52). I have even read that Cicero (*de Nat Deo III,* 22) describes the crater, yet his actual words are far from clear (see, for all these quotes, Ukert: *Ueber die Insel Lemnos und den Mosychlos.* Allgemeine Geographische Ephemeriden. vol. 39, 1812, pp. 361-386; and my note 2).

When, starting in the Renaissance, European travelers began to explore Lemnos (then still part of the Turkish Empire), they looked hard for the Lemnos volcano but could find no trace of it. This did not deter them from identifying various hills they saw on the island with the enigmatic Mosychlos. Early in the 19th century, several theories were advanced to account for the curious fact of the missing volcano, and it was thought that it had become extinct at the time of Alexander the Great, or that it had sunk below the waves during an earthquake in the time of Antonine after having been active for 1,200 years. Actually, geologists today deny any recent volcanic activity on the island (that includes Roman times, too). While the ancients reported almost continuous eruptions, there just weren't any.

As Walter Leaf (ed., *The Iliad.* London: Macmillan 1900) comments: "the 'Lemnian Fire' on Mount Mosychlos (...) is commonly taken to mean that Mosychlos was a volcano. But the present state of the island forbids the assumption of volcanic agency, and the fire was probably only a jet of natural gas. ... The supposed disappearance of the 'volcano' ... is geologically untenable."

The famous German geographer and explainer of geographical myths, Richard Henning (*Altgriechische Sagengestalten als Persionifikation von Erdfeuern und vulkanischen Vorgängen.* JDAI 54, 1939, p. 230ff.) supported the gas hypothesis. I haven't been able to get hold of a copy of his papers, but an internet search showed that additional earth fires (natural gas flames from the ground) were known from the Lykian Olympus, in Arcadia, and from the river Anas at Apollonia in Epirus.

Still, the Lemnos volcano might not even have been a "jet of natural gas." Modern thought tends so see the whole reporting of eruptions and lava flows by the classical writers as a misunderstanding. Lemnos was the first place where Hephaistos, the Greek smithy god, was venerated—probably by a temple fire, or a temple close to the smithy fires of the famous ironsmiths of the island. When the Greeks later discovered Mt. Etna on Sicily, they moved Hephaistos' home there, and possibly thought that, because Mt. Etna was a volcano, so must have been Lemnos. The Romans called Hephaistos Vulcan, so an island dedicated to Hephaistos was "a volcanic island," even if it had no natural, fire-spouting mountain. Later, the island of the god Volcanus, or "volcanic island" was thought to be identical with what we now call a volcano, and Renaissance experts—well into the 19th century, actually, and maybe the ancient Romans well before them—took this dedication literally to mean an actual volcano.

Conclusion

Although an anomalist should never say never, I am confident there is no new and previously unrecorded natural phenomenon behind these out-of-place volcanoes. For one, no mysterious or debatable geological anomaly has ever been found on Raasay, near Freiburg, or in Antrim in Ireland, or at any of the other sites were no normal explanation for the reported events immediately suggest itself. While a UFO might land and leave no trace, or a lake monster might surface and the photo comes out blurred, it is highly unlikely, or rather impossible, that a volcano might erupt, produce lava flows but leave no trace, no crater, nor volcanic rock for us to see today. Therefore, these cases cannot have been real volcanoes.

Yet my term "out-of-place-volcanoes" is, it appears, an umbrella term for many different kind of phenomena. Among the instances are geological phenomena, some related to volcanism, others not. Some are clearly honest misinterpretations, others outright hoaxes.

Possible explanations of these volcanoes as natural phenomena include:

- a thunderstorm hovering over a mountain top at the time of an earthquake or seismic shock,
- cave-ins with the resulting clouds of debris and dust forming a cloud pillar
- landslides,
- artesian fountains, mud volcanoes and geyser-like phenomena,
- outburst of inflammable natural gas, (3)

- sub-surface coal deposits ignited by lightning, (4)
- and transposition of real volcanic events onto a more familiar scene by writers of broadsheets.

The reports range from the imaginary to the fantastic, to the semi-real and real geological phenomena, some related to volcanism (such as mud volcanoes), some not (such as caverns caving in, or landslides). Out-of-place volcanoes also warn against a too literal interpretation of eyewitness reports and accounts in old chronicles. As the Chamonix example shows, even natives who know their land well may be grossly mislead about what they see in their natural environment. To rely on eyewitness testimony is always to rely on the interpretation of things by eyewitnesses—and it would be as foolish to assume that all these volcanic eruptions were "real" but left no trace. It may, I feel, be similarly unreasonable to rely on old chronicles and eyewitnesses regarding other phenomena, such as UFOs and water monsters.

Notes

1. Although not really part of the problem discussed here, it should be noted that there is some scientific speculation that the bed of a reservoir in the Ticino Valley, the lago di Tremorgio in Switzerland, may actually be a meteor crater: K. Bächtiger: "Lago di Tremorgio (Canton Ticino) — A Meteorite Impact Crater in the Swiss Alps?" *Cellular and Molecular Life Sciences* (CMLS), vol. 32, Nr. 9, September 1976, pp. 1102-1104. This opens the whole field of doubtful meteorite craters that are accepted by some geologists and rejected by others. Perfect examples are the Sirenete crater field in central Italy with about thirty depressions, which is identified by some as a meteorite crater from the time of Emperor Constantine but believed by others to be an artificial medieval pond for watering cows, or even a World War II shell crater; and the so-called chain of craters from the Chiemgau impact in southeast Germany, which some pioneering geologists have identified as the Phaeton impact of Greek myth (and the time "heaven fell on the Celts," from Alexander the Great) but which are thought to be just glacial phenomena by conventional geologists. Vienna catastrophists Alexander and Edith Tollmann claim in their book *Und die Sintflut gab es doch* (1993) that an asteroid crashed to earth and caused the universal deluge; they have identified one of the impact sites as Köfels in Tyrol, while conventional geologists regard this only as a common rock slide, yet of massive proportions.
2. Among others, these classical sources are usually mentioned in favor of the Lemnos volcano: "Volcanus... is the son of... Jupiter and of Juno, and is fabled to have been the master of a smithy at Lemnos." (Cicero, De Natura Deorum III. 22) "Nor [does a] greater noise [come] from the Lemnian caves when Mulciber [Hephaistos] amid his flames forges the

aegis and makes chaste gifts for Pallas." (Statius, *Silvae* 3.1.130) "From the firepeak rock of Lemnos the two Kabeiroi in arms ... two sons of Hephaistos whom Thrakian Kabeiro had borne to the heavenly smith, Alkon and Eurymedon well skilled at the forge." (Nonnus, *Dionysiaca* 14.17) "Lemnos, Vulcanus' island." (Ovid, *Metamorphoses* 2. 757; 13. 314 ff)

3. Tongues of fire issuing from the earth are so often reported that I have listed only a few instances here, others may be found in John Michell's and Robert Rickard's: *Rough Guide to Unexplained Phenomena*. Rough Guides, London 2007 (p. 181: the Abbé Girolamo Leoni de Ceneda was terrified by a flame bursting from the ground in a village near Venice, 1713), and William R. Corliss (*Lightning, Auroras, Nocturnal Lights and related luminous phenomena*. Glen Arm, MD: Sourcebook Project 1982, p. 172f), such as the jets of fire reported on 5 June 1902 from the mud of a shallow channel near the shore at Blundellsands, Liverpool, the flames at Harlech, Wales, from the winter of 1694, and the flames from the ground at Kittery Point, Maine, on 1 September 1905. As these are single flames, often lasting only for seconds or minutes, they may have their origin in natural gas discharges rather than in out-of-place volcanoes.

4. A fine example of this is the Brennender Berg, the burning mountain, at Dudweiler in the German Saarland. A subterranean coal layer began to burn in 1668 when a shepherd ignited it by accident, and it has burned ever since, even becoming a sight to see in the region. All attempts to quench it have failed, and smoke still issues from the ground. Johann Wolfgang von Goethe visited the burning mountain in June 1770 and wrote about it in his autobiography *Out of my life: Poetry and Truth* (vol. 2, bk 10, 1812). An American example of this phenomenon is the burning coal at Centralia, Pennsylvania.

Ulrich Magin, born 1962, lives in Southern Germany. His main interests are cryptozoology, marine forteana, ufology, and geomancy. He has written books on all these subjects, the most recent one on sightings of monsters in the Italian alpine lakes.

HETLERVILLE:
OMENS IN THE SKY?
BY DWIGHT WHALEN

Hetlerville, Pennsylvania, should be famous. Or if not famous, at least well known to aficionados of accounts of anomalous phenomena. Instead, the story of what happened there in 1914, far from being the stuff of legend, has been lost to historical memory. In the annals of the mysterious, not so much as a footnote gives it mention. Even in Hetlerville today, and communities nearby, the story of the aerial apparitions seen there at the dawn of the First World War is known to hardly anyone. As suddenly as the mystery burst into the night sky above this patch of Pennsylvania farm country and into the headlines of area newspapers, the story vanished, its hasty death and burial coming at the hands of a plausible-sounding explanation. But when examined closely, the proposed solution falls well short of explaining the whole affair. The Hetlerville Mystery is mysterious still.

I stumbled upon the story in the same way others in Hetlerville and surrounding towns and villages learned of it long ago—in the pages of a newspaper. In my case, the paper was a back file of the *Niagara Falls Journal* (Niagara Falls, NY), dated 31 July 1914. Browsing old newspapers in search of the strange and forgotten is a pastime of mine, so when I came across this page-one item I was immediately intrigued:

"Strange Omens in Sky Worry These People
"Berwick, Pa., July 31 - With three responsible residents of Hetlerville telling today of strange pictures they saw outlined in the skies, the superstitious in that vicinity are looking for some calamity, just what, they do not know.

"Harry Hudleson was returning home from Nescopeck when he says he was startled to see visibly outlined in the heavens a picture of an immense house filled with children dressed in white with a black band on the arm of each. As he stood looking, the children came out of the house in columns of two, dividing at the door, with each column forming in an opposite direction.

"Mrs. Rush Lutz, a neighbor, had a similar experience. She saw an immense house in the sky, like a picture thrown on the screen, with the wind waving the canvas."

While an obviously truncated report, I had all I needed to start digging for more, starting with a Google Earth map check. Berwick, the place in the dateline, is twenty-four miles southwest of Wilkes-Barre, Pennsylvania. Hetlerville is three miles southwest of Berwick, bordered on the north by the Susquehanna River and on the south by the looming Nescopeck ridge. Ten miles to the west, across the Susquehanna, lies the county seat of Bloomsburg. Beyond the big ridge, the rolling mountains of eastern Pennsylvania's anthracite coal country unfold. Hetlerville, part of Mifflin Township in Columbia County, is a farming community.

Curious to know what the Berwick press reported, and what other newspapers in the Hetlerville area had to say about the mysterious "omens in the sky," I hired two research assistants, Mrs. Winifred M. Neufer of Berwick, and David L. Klees of Harrisburg, the state capitol, where a newspaper archive is held at the State Library of Pennsylvania. I asked them to search newspaper records of Columbia County for the period from late July through early August 1914. Both uncovered fascinating articles.

As I expected to learn, Hetlerville itself had no paper. Unfortunately, although Berwick did have a paper, the *Enterprise*, in 1914, no copies from that period survive. As Mr. Klees quaintly put it, "the mice got them."

Mrs. Neufer visited the library of Bloomsburg University, "the only place near Berwick that has old newspapers on microfilm." There she found the following front-page story in *The Morning Press* of Bloomsburg, Thursday, 30 July 1914:

"Strange Visions in Sky, Hetlerville Folks Have Seen
Sight of Immense House With Marching Children One Saw,
Another an Angel
Building by Another
Stories Told by Responsible Parties and the Superstitious Are
Aroused
"With one Hetlerville resident seeing in the skies a picture vividly outlined, showing an immense house filled with children, dressed in white and with each child having a band of black on the arm; with yet another seeing an immense house and the third the form of an angel,

those who are superstitious in that end of the country are wondering what will come next.

"Were the stories not told by entirely responsible people little credence would be placed in the tales that are told, but the facts are such that those who know the parties concerned do not doubt them for a minute.

"Harry Hudleson was returning to his home in Hetlerville from Nescopeck when his attention was attracted to the sky and he was startled to see a picture vividly outlined in the heavens, of an immense house, filled with children who were dressed in white, with a black band upon the arm of each.

"And as Hudleson stood looking, he declares the children came out of the house in columns of two, dividing at the door, with each column going in an opposite direction.

"The sight was too plain for him to be mistaken and he was not dreaming, Mr. Hudleson declares, with emphasis. Greatly impressed by the sight he told the family but said little elsewhere until on the following Sunday, Mrs. Rush Lutz, a resident of that place, related a similar and equally remarkable experience.

"Mrs. Lutz went into the yard at eleven o'clock Saturday night to take from the line the clothes she had washed that day when she also was attracted by the appearance of the sky. An immense house was shown vividly with an effect that she describes as wind waving through a rye field or a picture would be on a screen if the canvas was being blown about. Mr. Lutz is also equally positive. She wondered at the phenomena and hurried into the house. The sight remained for ten minutes or more.

"The description Mrs. Lutz gives of the building she saw pictured in the sky and that of Mr. Hudleson are remarkably similar.

"Neither offered any solution and together with everyone to whom they told their experiences both were greatly mystified. That some sign was meant was the usual interpretation with thoughts at first of some terrible happening or disaster. Still another, Pearl Pursel, declares that she saw in the heavens the form of an angel.

"A possible solution is that it was a mirage. On the ocean and on a desert the reflection is frequently seen in the skies of objects far away. This is explained by the particular state of the atmosphere and the conflicting air currents that give a reflection.

"That it is a mirage that each of the Hetlerville residents saw is a possibility and unusual weather of this summer may give some substantiation. Whatever the phenomena there is no doubt of its being full and thrilling reality to the persons mentioned and credited generally by the residents of Hetlerville and section adjacent as the occurrences are being widely related, with general wonder expressed."

Leaving aside the mirage speculation for now, the image of the huge house reportedly seen in the heavens by Mrs. Lutz appeared "Saturday night," i.e., 25 July. *The Morning Press* didn't give a date for Harry Hudleson's sighting but that it also took place that same Saturday night is implied. However, this is contradicted by the *The Morning News* of nearby Danville, Friday, 31 July. Its report, headlined "Villagers See Visions in Sky," essentially a verbatim copy of the *Press*'s article from the day before, adds one noteworthy detail: The Hudleson sighting is said to have occurred on "Friday night last," i.e., 24 July. If accurate, maybe this detail was cribbed from another paper, perhaps the Berwick *Enterprise*.

A few days after their stories appeared in the Bloomsburg paper, both witnesses came forward again with more details of their sightings, encouraged, no doubt, by word that residents of Scottown, an outlying district of Bloomsburg, had also seen peculiar sights in the sky recently. From page one of *The Morning Press*, Monday, 3 August:

"Scottown Folks, Too, See Strange Sights in Skies
Their Experience Was Much Like That of Mrs. Lutz, of Hetlerville
Phenomena Continues
Girl Who Saw the Angel Feared Vision Was an Omen
"There is almost anything to be seen in the skies up in Columbia County these days if you look at the right time!

"Following the experiences of Hetlerville folks, as given in these columns the other day, Scottown residents declare they likewise saw strange sights and in large numbers during the latter part of last week [when] they viewed the phenomena.

"The sights they saw nearly duplicate those of Mrs. Rush Lutz, who went into details in discussing the phenomena, after her first experiences got into print. Said she: 'The light that I saw in the sky made it light enough in the yard for me to see to wring out clothes. It was from an object in the sky that appeared as bright almost as the sun. I can't explain it and don't try to. Anyone who has a solution to explain it [?]. The light was there. It was the strangest thing that I ever saw or expect to.'

"Mrs. Lutz spoke with an emphasis that showed her to have been profoundly moved by the strange experience. She continued, 'I had some clothes to wring out. I lighted the lantern and lamp to go to the well and when I was working the light appeared. It was light enough for me to work. As I looked across the fields I could see the wheat stubble as plainly as in the day time and every object in the fields. I looked with awe at the heavens. It seemed to start at a point over Nescopeck hill and swing across the heavens until it got to a point near the mountain and would go out, reappear and swing back. It did this three times across the skies. I ran into the house and upstairs and awakened my husband. It was a dark night. The sky was filled with stars and there was no moon. When the light disappeared it was perfectly dark. The light appeared to be like the front of a house. It was there a good many minutes. I was not fooled, was not dreaming and my eyes are not bad. I was thinking of nothing but my washing and would not have noticed the sky but for the fact that it grew so light about me that my lantern and lamp were not needed. I don't know what caused it or what it means, but it was there. God only knows.'

"Harry Hudleson who saw the mansion in the sky and the smiling children, was driving to his home in Hetlerville from Willow Grove when he declares he saw the strange sight to which reference was previously made.

"Going into more detail, Hudleson declares the sight he saw was that of a building outlined in a blaze of white. Then appeared two children, one entering and the other coming from the building. Both were dressed in white, although the bows in which their sashes were tied were different. Alongside the house were apparently thousands of children, each smiling. The faces of two became so distinct, he declared, that he would know them again. Fearing he would be ridiculed, he told only his wife and not until the Lutz and Hudleson families met, when Mrs. Lutz related her experience did he make known the sight he had seen.

"Miss Pearl Pursel, aged 16, who lives beyond Nescopeck and who saw the form of an angel, was deeply affected by the sight. She took it as an omen and couldn't get it off her mind. When she saw the strange sight of the skies she told no one other than her mother, likewise fearing ridicule.

"Peter Eddinger, of West Berwick, declares that in the daytime he saw outlined in the skies an exact reproduction of a flag of perfect bars of black, red and a tint that resembled a light bluish green. There was not a cloud in the sky at the time and upon going home [he] looked in the encyclopedia to see if there was any nation that had a flag like it, but found none.

"That there has been some phenomena in the skies seems likely, for Scottown citizens whose attention was directed to the flashes that resembled those seen by Mrs. Lutz declare there could be no mistake as to what they had seen with their own eyes."

The Morning News of Danville dutifully ran the identical story, without embellishments, the following day.

Mrs. Rush Lutz and Harry Hudleson, both of Hetlerville, were neighbors. Each witnessed something extraordinary in the dark night sky independent of the other, possibly on adjacent nights. Considering that they went to the press with their stories only after comparing notes, it's remarkable that their accounts differ as much as they do. Beyond agreeing about a bright light in the sky that, in some way unexplained, presented an image of a huge house brightly outlined, they have nothing else in common. It would appear from this that neither witness influenced the other's testimony unduly.

Mrs. Lutz was most impressed by the brightness of the light—"as bright almost as the sun." She said it shone from "an object in the sky," and the light flooded her farm so brightly that she no longer needed a lantern to work by, and could see every detail on her property clearly, as if it were daylight. The illumination lasted some minutes. Her husband saw it too. In neither of the two accounts she gave to *The Morning Press* did she mention seeing children or any other figures in the sky.

Harry Hudleson, on the other hand, did see children. Lots of them. He saw them, he said, when his attention was drawn to a bright light in the sky, "a blaze of white" that, halo-like, outlined the image of a huge building, apparently a house. The children appeared to number thousands, and were all dressed in white. They marched out of the house and formed up in columns on opposite sides, said the *Press*'s original report, and the children wore black armbands. In his second account to the *Press*, Hudleson held to his claim of seeing thousands of children in white surrounding a big house, but spoke of only one child entering the house and another exiting it, and that the "bows in which their sashes were tied" were a different color. To top everything off, Hudleson claimed that, not only could he see all the children smiling, but the faces of two of them appeared so distinct that he felt he could recognize them again! Small wonder he didn't share his story with anyone but his wife before learning what his neighbor, Mrs. Lutz, had seen.

Before considering possible explanations, why were the Lutz and Hudleson sightings so different? If the Danville *Morning News* got it right, and Hudleson's experience occurred on Friday, not Saturday as did Mrs. Lutz's, that would explain the differences, even if it explained nothing else. On the other hand, if they both saw the same phenomenon on Saturday, they would have been viewing it from different, albeit nearby, locations, and therefore from different vantage points. Recalling that Mrs. Lutz at one point returned to the house to wake up her husband to come out to see the strange glow, it might have been during that interval when she wasn't looking skyward that the throng of children Hudleson saw appeared.

Now, others were coming forward saying they too had seen strange things in the heavens. Occurring "the latter part of last week," this would place the sightings between Thursday, 30 July, and Saturday, 1 August. Scottown residents had allegedly seen flashes and sights that "nearly duplicated" what Mrs. Lutz had seen. One saw what she took to be an angel; another, a spectral flag in the sky in broad daylight. Witnesses were said to be deeply impressed with what they saw, and regarded the mysterious visions with superstitious awe and dread.

What in the world was going on in Columbia County? Residents didn't have long to wait for an answer. *The Morning Press* of Bloomsburg, Wednesday, 4 August, declared the mystery solved. Next to a wide page-one column announcing that the German Army was advancing on Paris, and other alarming war bulletins, appeared the following:

"Ssh! Secret's Out; It Wasn't An Omen
Strange Sights in Heavens Explained But Angels Are Still There
"The Scotttown folks who thought they saw strange things in the sky really did; so did some of the Hetlerville people and so did some of the others.

"The fellows who have been laughing at you have been the foolish ones, even though what you saw was not an omen—the war that is on casting its shadow before.

"The lights you saw were the rays from a powerful searchlight that is part of the advertising equipment of a carnival company now holding forth in Ashland. Now, what do you think of that?

"E. W. Stiner, who lives in the Roaring Creek valley, and who has been in Berwick, saw the lights upon his return home; saw them night after night, and then sought the explanation.

"No one has been able, however, to account for the angels in the heavens; they're probably still there."

The Morning News of Danville, 8 August, ran a reworked version of the same report but worded more soberly, and mentioned only one angel, as originally reported: "No one has been able, however, to account for the angel in the sky."

A carnival's promotional searchlight. Was this the source of the aerial apparitions? Indeed, a carnival had been operating in the region, and it did have a searchlight to attract attention. During the period of the Lutz-Hudleson sightings, "Reithoffer's United Shows" had been operating at a place called Pottsville, south of Hetlerville, in neighboring Schuykill County. The carnival certainly could have moved next to Ashland, where the *Press* of August 4 placed it. Ashland is a borough that bestrides Columbia and Schuykill Counties, about 10 miles northwest of Pottsville. The newspaper records I was given to examine tell of no other carnival or searchlight operating in the area at that time. There are no extant Ashland papers from 1914.

An ad in *The Pottsville Republican*, July 23, announced:

"Reithoffer's United Shows
One Week - July 20 to 25ᵗʰ
At Dolan's Park,
Pottsville
Show carries
- $20,000 Carousel.
- Trip to Mars.
- Motodrome, in which the "Flying Dutchman" and "Cyclone Kelley," mounted on 16 horse power Motorcycles, run a race at rate of 90 miles an hour. These men defy death.
- Great Arctic show from North Pole educating young and old.
- All other kinds of Amusements, clean and refined for children, ladies and gentlemen.
- The Free Attraction - Smallest Horse in the World, carried with this show for two years in a Suitcase.
Two Performances Daily
Afternoon at 2 o'clock;
Evening at 7 o'clock."

The same issue of the *Republican* also carried this item:

"Big Crowds at Carnival
"Big crowds are the order every evening at the Reithoffer carnival, which is being held at Dolan's Park this week. The shows are all clean and above criticism and are popular among women and children, as well

as men. The big searchlight is attracting attention as it flashes continually through the sky in every direction."

On the date Mrs. Lutz encountered the mysterious light, 25 July, the carnival was still in Pottsville, 25 July being its closing date. Mrs. Lutz said the light appeared over "Nescopeck hill," the big ridge, or mountain, abutting Hetlerville on the south. Hetlerville's elevation is about 900 feet. The ridge looms about 500 feet above that, blocking any view of Pottsville which, although also 900 feet high, is 25 miles and many interverning hills away. While a spotlight's beam shining up into the sky at Pottsville might have been visible from Hetlerville, the light that illuminated Mrs. Lutz, if it came from a spotlight, couldn't have come from the Pottsville valley.

Reithoffer's carnival evidently next moved to Ashland, a bit southwest of Hetlerville, a little over 15 miles away. But when did the spotlight arrive? Suppose it had been sent to Ashland and turned on there late on the night of 25 July. That would match the time and date of Mrs. Lutz's strange sighting. However, Ashland's elevation is only 100 feet higher than Hetlerville's, which places it several hundred feet lower than Nescopeck Mountain. In other words, in a valley, just like Pottsville, posing the same obvious problem. Yet, a carnival with a searchlight clearly was in the Pottsville-Ashland area 25 July when Mrs. Lutz beheld a dazzling light above the mountain, an illumination that bathed her in a bright glow. She described a light that swept across the sky "until it got to a point near the mountain and would go out, reappear and swing back. It did this three times..." If this was the Reithoffer carnival searchlight, its operator was a long way from the Ashland fairground.

Having never been to Hetlerville, never eyeballed Nescopeck Mountain, I can't swear that no elevations are visible beyond the mountain from the fields below, points from which a spotlight could be shone down onto Hetlerville. But I'm confident there are no such vantage points. Zooming in on the landmass via Google Earth and viewing it from various angles in Hetlerville, particularly points farthest back from the mountain, I failed to discern a single high point beyond the crest, only sky. Nescopeck Mountain is one imposing ridge.

But before I'd realized Ashland wasn't the answer, and still thinking that maybe the light Mrs. Lutz saw did come from there, as *The Morning Press* claimed, I wondered: Could a searchlight shining from 15 miles away cast a glow with anything like the brilliance of the light that flooded the Lutz farm?

Bob Meza is an expert on searchlights. He has actually restored a

WWII carbon arc searchlight. According to his website (google Bob's Searchlight Page), his searchlight is one of many "produced from 1932 to 1944 by General Electric and Sperry Gyroscope for the U.S. Military as Anti-Aircraft Searchlight Units." Production ended with the advent of radar. I shared Mrs. Lutz's account with him and asked if a searchlight, specifically one from the 1914 era, could have been the source of light she described.

"Yes," he replied, "a searchlight on a hilltop could light her up like day from fifteen miles away. The action of the light does sound like a searchlight. Some operator messing around with the light, pointing it down instead of up."

But he added a note of caution: "She says the light came from the sky and not a hilltop. I would think she would know the area and know if the light source came from the top of a hill."

Fair point. She did say the light came from "an object in the sky." But she'd been looking toward the skyline formed by the ridge. It's easy to imagine that, as Mrs. Lutz peered at the brightly glowing light, the distinction between the horizon and the sky above could have been obscured in the glow. A mysterious beam of light shining downward through a low bank of clouds or fog that momentarily took the shape of a large house could possibly explain the weird scene Mrs. Lutz and Harry Hudleson agreed they saw. Except that there was no mention of clouds in their accounts. To the contrary, Mrs. Lutz said the night was moonless and full of stars.

Nevertheless, the Reithoffer searchlight—sent to Ashland late Saturday night, 25 July, the driver getting lost near Hetlerville, turning on the spotlight to help get his bearings in the dark?—remains Suspect Number One as the most likely source of the unusual lights seen in the skies over Columbia County.

Interestingly, Reithoffer Shows, Inc., founded in 1896, is still in business today. Its rides and attractions appear April through November "up and down the eastern seaboard and as far west as Missouri, playing the nation's best fairs and festivals," according to the Shows' website. But my email inquiries to Reithoffer Shows about their 1914 season in Pennsylvania drew no response. (Their searchlight aside, what was that "horse in a suitcase" all about?)

To the south of Bloomsburg, in a place called Mount Carmel, much closer to Ashland, reports came from there, too, of a searchlight as well as "peculiar objects" in the sky. First, the *Mount Carmel Item*, 29 July:

"Mysterious Search Light Has Attention

"A high powered search light cast its rays across the heavens last night and created considerable interest in Mount Carmel. It is thought that the light was cast from Ashland."

The *Item* proposed its own solution to the mystery, August 5:

"An Explanation of the Mysterious Heavenly Sights

"On Thursday evening [July 30] Mount Carmel again saw bright light[s] in the south-eastern horizon. They were very peculiar and resembled different objects. It has been reported that people living near Nescopeck have seen angels, children and houses in the sky..."

The *Item*, referencing the *Lancaster Almanac*, offered the star Sirius, the brightest star in the sky, as the culprit. Sirius is low in the southern sky in mid-northern latitudes, rising in the southeast and setting in the southwest. Close as it is to the horizon, its light passes through more of Earth's atmosphere than the light of most other stars. Changes in air density and temperature can cause its bright light to twinkle, change color, or flash. It has sometimes been mistaken for a UFO, but never, to my knowledge, for a large crowd of smiling children, etc.

Harry Hudleson, in his view of marching, thronging children, must have beheld a spectacle that filled much of the sky, if he could clearly make out such small details as armbands, smiles, and recognizably visible faces. Too, whereas other observers reportedly saw only a single image—a house, a flag, an angel—Hudleson was granted a view of what sounds like multiple images in procession, as though he were watching a motion picture or slide show in the sky. It must have been a staggering sight. But even if Tom Swift were working for the Reithoffer carnival that summer, and the "searchlight" was actually the largest stereopticon ever invented, it would still require a reflecting surface of dense clouds upon which to project its huge slide images into the sky. Again, Mrs. Lutz mentioned no clouds. Likewise, the "flag" seen by Peter Eddinger appeared when "there was not a cloud in the sky." And it was daylight. No searchlight can be blamed for that one.

Recalling the historical significance of the days of late July 1914, could the visions described have had as much to do with collective anxiety as anything else? The Hetlerville phenomena, it can't be overlooked, took place precisely during the days when the fate of the world, and the deaths of millions, was being sealed by events unfolding in Europe.

Austria-Hungary declared war on Serbia, 28 July. Nation after nation, treaty-bound to defend its allies, tumbled into the maelstrom of war virtually overnight.

Against that background, it has to be asked if "war nerves" played a role in the visions seen. Signs in the heavens, folklore holds, often foretell dark events, and whatever else was going on overhead in the Hetlerville area, talk of war had been in the air for weeks.

Following the assassination of Franz Ferdinand, Archduke of Austria, and his wife in Sarajevo, 28 June, by a Serbian extremist, European powers tilted toward war. But after the expected saber rattling, and days passed without military reprisal, most of the world was lulled into believing diplomacy would avert catastrophe. Throughout most of July there was little talk of war in the press. Thus, when war did break out, 28 July, Americans, like most people, were taken by surprise. But no war hysteria ensued: The U.S. was a neutral power for most of the war, maintaining its neutrality until joining the Allied cause against Germany in 1917.

The good farmers of Hetlerville and their neighbors would not have been overly anxious about developments in the Balkans as of July 24-25, when the visions started. If any anxieties prevailed, they would have concerned crops, livestock, the harvest, and when heads turned skyward it would have been to keep an eye on the weather. Tensions in Europe would hardly have been a distraction.

Interestingly, by the wildest coincidence the war would soon produce another story of a mysterious something-seen-in-the-sky—this time, over the bloody battlefields of Belgium. Stories appeared in the British press, and all throughout the war, of the "Angel of Mons," a spectral figure whose appearance rallied retreating British forces, and paralyzed the pursuing Germans with fear, by its awesome and mesmerizing appearance in the sky. Or so the tale usually went. But in *The Angel of Mons: Phantom Soldiers and Ghostly Guardians* (Wiley; 2004), author David Clarke concludes the story was a myth. He could find no firsthand account from any survivor of the retreat at Mons to substantiate the Angel story, or any supernatural variant of it.

The story, in fact, had its origin in a work of fiction.

Ironically, while the Angel of Mons legend is famous, despite the lack of first-hand eyewitness testimony, the "Angel of Hetlerville," seen at the advent of the war, has been forgotten, even though a named witness at the time, Pearl Pursel, came forward. The sight of the supposed angel left her awestruck. But alas, that is all we know. The *Press* didn't press her for details. We don't know what the angel looked like, if it was seen in daytime or at night, etc. A few days later, giddy with relief, the paper blamed the whole series of strange visions on the carnival searchlight.

Something more than a searchlight had to be involved. This leads to a final possibility: temperature inversions. Ordinarily, air at ground level is warmer than air higher up. When this is reversed, as when lake and sea surfaces during warm spring days are colder than the air above, light is refracted, or bent, downward by the denser cold air where the contrasting air masses meet. This can produce what is called a "superior mirage," superior because the ghostly image looms above, not below, the mirrored subject. Even things beyond the horizon can be seen if conditions are favorable. More common in polar regions, superior mirages, when they form at moderate latitudes, are usually less stable, less defined, and can create enormous distortions. A distant shoreline can appear to tower like a castle. Or a house like an enormous mansion.

The waving, shimmering quality of mirages is compatible with one feature of Mrs. Lutz's report: "An immense house was shown vividly with an effect that she describes as wind waving through a rye field or a picture would be on a screen if the canvas was being blown about." The colored bars Peter Eddinger took to resemble a flag could have been a trick of the atmosphere, too.

Yet, the Lutz-Hudleson "mirages," if that's what they were, appeared accompanied by brilliant light, long after sunset. While a mirage can appear day or night, and a superior mirage can show objects, including the sun, well beyond the horizon, "the inversion layer," according to the entry for "Superior Mirage" in Wikipedia, "must have just the right temperature gradient over the whole distance to make this possible." In this case, over a distance of two thousand miles, as the sun, if that was the light source, was then setting on the west coast. Can a mirage "travel" that far?

Superior mirages are most often seen over bodies of water. They are less common over land and of shorter duration there, generally. The original *Press* article of 30 July spoke of "unusual weather this summer," and ventured that mirage phenomena was the source of the visions before later embracing the searchlight solution. Mirages certainly can't be ruled out. In fact, in the absence of a better explanation, mirages appear to be the most likely source of the astounding images. Maybe the carnival searchlight, interacting with superior mirages, provides the fullest answer to the mystery, if less than a complete one: The optical physics of mirage production would still have to account for how a feature as small as a human face, as opposed to large distant objects and landscapes, could be seen to loom in clear focused detail in the sky, if we take Harry Hudleson's testimony at, well, face value.

The area bordered by Berwick, Bloomsburg, Hetlerville, and Mount Carmel is, geographically speaking, quite small. Despite this, reports and rumors of strange apparitions in the sky were confined, apparently, to this limited area over a sustained period of a days. What atmospheric phenomena could have prevailed for that long, producing the phantasmagoria of images in the heavens day and night—a great crowd of children, clear facial images, the facade of a huge building, the form of an angel, a flag, and who knows what else? Superior mirages and their shape-shifting acts don't usually stick around over land for weeklong engagements.

In the end, more striking than the Hetlerville visions themselves is the fact that they occurred when they did, and depicted what they did. To me, that is the greater wonder. Regardless of what caused the sky visions, one could reasonably interpret the reported images, in the aggregate, as indeed symbolic of events to come: augurs of the Great War, manifesting with exquisite timing.

As I see it, the large house stands for security and order in the world, the edifice of human civilization. The throng of smiling children in white, from Hudleson's vision, represents innocent youth. Their emerging from the house—leaving comfort, security, and peace behind. Their marching off into two opposing columns—the movement of opponents, aligning for conflict. Alternately, as Hudleson's second version has it, the one where two children pass each other in opposite directions, one entering the house, the other exiting—opposing energies of peace and war. The countless children wearing black armbands tell of mourning and death, and in great numbers. The flag means nations are involved, and so it's war. As to the angel reported, I can't accept, in the context of what became the vast slaughterhouse of the Great War, a heavenly being as a symbol of hope. Rather, if anything, it was the biblical "Angel of Death."

Others may read "the signs" differently, or see in the ghostly images nothing more than highly extraordinary mirage phenomena dancing in the beam of a searchlight. Or some other wonder no less marvelous and equally unlikely. The only certain conclusion now, a century later, is that a complete understanding of what occurred is beyond all reach. In Columbia County today, a woman named Bonnie Farver serves as Executive Director of the Columbia County Historical and Genealogical

Society, and unofficial historian of Mifflin/Mifflin Township. I emailed her the "Strange Visions" clipping from *The Morning Press* of 30 July 1914, and asked her if the story is recalled in Hetlerville today. She said it's not. In fact, she told me she'd never heard of it before I brought it to her attention, even though she "grew up in Hetlerville about a mile from Harry." Harry Hudleson married Minnie Mowery, a sister to Bonnie's grandfather. Referring to the view beyond Nescopeck Mountain, she is firm: "I know you can't see any hills from Hetlerville."

Bonnie added a couple of more details, too, which I appreciate. Mrs. Lutz, she told me, was Margaret Elizabeth (Rush) Lutz, born 6 May 1866, and died 3 June 1943. Harry Hudleson was born 9 August 1874, and died 24 May 1964. Both are buried in Mifflin Cemetery, a few miles outside of Hetlerville.

Dwight Whalen is a writer and researcher who lives in Niagara Falls, Ontario. His articles have appeared in Fate *magazine,* Fortean Times, *the* INFO Journal, *and other publications. He is the author of War Christmas, a compilation of war letters of Niagara servicemen written during the Christmas seasons of the First and Second World Wars.*

A LESSON IN SPECULATIVE ARCHAEOLOGY:
THE CASE OF THE MOCHÉ
BY CAMERON MATTHEW BLOUNT

In the conservative world of archaeological methodology, the traditional approach toward analyzing artistic representation can be summarized as: when all else fails, blame the gods. In other words, when looking at an "unrecognizable" piece of artwork, if it can't be conveniently explained in a way that fits with existing evidence or theories, the subject matter must be mythological. This approach is applied across the spectrum of archaeology, from Stone Age hunter-gatherer settlements to Civil War era battlefields. The advantage of this approach is clear: by conveniently pigeon-holing material that cannot be explained by conventional means, we avoid the need to answer the difficult and controversial questions these items pose.

As a young student considering a career in archaeology, I was blindsided by this approach while taking an undergraduate course on the ancient cultures of Peru. The instructor was Christopher B. Donnan, a world renowned expert (if not *the* expert) on the archaeology of South America. Donnan's work has featured on the cover of *National Geographic*, in the pages of *Archaeology*, and his many books can be found in both academic libraries and popular bookstores all over the world. Donnan's true expertise is in the Moché, arguably the most advanced sub-culture that arose along one branch of the many Peruvian river valleys running down from the Andes during the time period between 100BC and 600AD. The proficiency of Moché artisans is striking. From recognizable human portraits to complicated depictions of food, plants, and animals, their artwork is a clear lens through which we can view the essence of Moché civilization.

As an archaeologist working along the Moché river valley, Donnan saw this proliferation of Moché culture come out of the ground firsthand. But one thing troubled him: along with the many pieces depicting everyday aspects of Moché life, there were also many representations of human sacrifice being carried out by strange figures that he could not readily identify. The more Donnan dug, the more he saw this depiction extend across all artistic mediums. The exact same scene of sacrifice adorned the walls of temples, pottery pieces, and textiles over and over again. In fact, the repetition became so frequent and so recognizable, Donnan assigned labels to the figures, "Figure A through Figure G," each label representing the distinct entities visible throughout the scene. And yet, although the remaining body of Moché art suggested a very literal translation of subject matter, Donnan could only conclude that the sacrificial scene had to be mythical. The odd headdresses, jewelry, and stylized armor did not fit neatly within any known cultural practices so it must be fanciful deities and representations of the complicated mythical beliefs of the Moché, which, unfortunately, have since been lost. There the matter was settled. With no chance of ever understanding the mythology of the Moché and with little hope of finding any proof to the contrary, the Moché sacrificial scene, so prevalent in art across the coastal regions of northern Peru, was cast off into the divine abyss.

But then, while digging in the ancient city of Sipan, Donnan made a startling discovery. Inside a tomb he unearthed a man who would later be dubbed the "Lord of Sipan." Here was an elite male buried with a headdress, weapons, jewelry, and body armor that matched exactly that of "Figure A" in the ubiquitous sacrificial scene of Moché artwork. The connection was clear: the sacrificial scene of the Moché, previously dismissed as myth, was a very real and very literal portrayal of an aspect of Moché life. Subsequently, in the many years of Peruvian excavations in the area, what followed was a catalog of objects and burials that bore out almost every aspect of the ritual scene. The amalgam of data spurred Donnan, perhaps grudgingly, to state: "Archaeological realism has been extremely useful in gauging the degree of realism in Moché iconography. For the most part, the material uncovered at Moché sites has demonstrated that nearly everything shown in the art is an accurate, though sometimes stylized, reading of the objects these people had available in their immediate environment."[1]

Now, keeping in mind what we know of Moché culture, let us look beyond the Moché river valley and examine ancient Peruvian culture as a whole. It is believed that the first advanced culture of ancient Peru arose out of the city center of Chavin de Huantar. The Chavin civilization is dated to approximately 900BC and, in consideration of its ancient origin, the region is believed to have held a very large population as well as a wide geographical sway of cultural influence. With its city hub located centrally amongst the Peruvian river valley system, Chavin de Huantar was ideally situated to spread its influence both northward and southward, its established practices for art, religion, and political beliefs emanating down river valleys throughout the region. To the north of Chavin de Huantar, the Moché culture developed. At the same time, in a river valley to the south, there arose the mysterious culture of the Nazca.

Compared side by side, even a cursory examination of the artwork of the Nazca and the Moché reveals that the artistic practices of the two cultures is closely tied. Stylistic depictions, as well as subject matter, are very similar. For example, the portrayal of trophy heads, or decapitated prisoners of war, are very prominent and treated in the same artistic manner in both the Moché and Nazca styles. Not incidentally, mummified heads discovered during excavations of both regions highlight the real existence of this practice. Snakes, birds, and vegetables are also prevalent, each piece a stylized but literal representation of the real thing. Adding weight to the relation between both cultures, we also know that these peoples had far-reaching trade routes and must have had regular contact with one another. Evidence for this contact is accounted for in the existence of animals and plants not native to the geographic region of each culture, species that must have been imported from considerable distances.

Yet, whereas the Moché have become known for their religious and political practices tied to ritual sacrifice, the Nazca are known for something entirely different: the Nazca Lines. Atop what is known as the Nazca Pampa, a large upraised mesa, are huge depictions of animals and geographic shapes that were only identified relatively recently because, strangely enough, the representations are only visible from the air. The sheer scope and artistic intricacy of the Nazca Lines is breathtaking. From stylistic depictions of whales, hummingbirds, and monkeys to trapezoids and triangles, the artistic subject matter is easily recognizable. That is, recognizable in every instance but one: the so called Nazca Astronaut. Lying on a hillside at the lower edge of the Nazca Pampa, the Nazca Astronaut is indeed a curious figure. There, almost traced as if by a child, is a strange humanoid representation. It has large, circular eyes and puffed out limbs, as if the depiction is wearing some sort of protective suit. The figure is unique (as far as we know) in Nazca iconography. Through today's cultural viewfinder this anomaly has been dubbed the "astronaut" because, indeed, it clearly resembles our culture's concept of a space traveller. What are we to make of it?

Not surprisingly, mainstream archaeologists pigeonholed the ancient astronaut as a mythical representation. This explanation flies in the face of everything that we know about the Nazca, their Moché brethren, and ancient Peruvian culture. The ancient Peruvians were a literal and artistic people who saw value in creating artistic representations of their immediate surroundings. This much we know as fact. The lessons of Professor Donnan and the Moché have taught us as much. What is also clear is that the Nazca had the artistic and technological sophistication to create exactly what it was that they meant to create. One only needs to look at the aerial photographs of the Nazca lines representing the monkey or whale (among others) to know that the Nazca could have drawn at the very least a recognizable human portrait had they the inclination to do so. But they did not, thereby leaving modern man with a troubling conclusion that he, collectively, has yet to make.

Stopping here for the moment, let us look at the wider picture one last time. Let us leave the Peruvian river valleys and examine the cave paintings of North Africa, the rock paintings in the Sego Canyon of Utah, or the early stone etchings of Val Comonica, Italy. Here we find depictions that we cannot understand: humans with glowing and bulbous heads, humanoid representations with large, circular eyes, and fiery chariots hovering in the sky. Should we also assume that these representations, just because we can't understand what they represent, are fantasy and not reality? Or is it the case that we can understand them but we purposefully choose not to accept the repercussions that such an acknowledgement would have on our early history as a species?

In the far reaches of humanity's past, prior to the adoption of nationalism, urbanism, and just about every other "ism" in existence today, our ancestors were simple beings. Over the course of human civilization, political and religious complexity evolved. The compendium of Greek mythology and Greek political organization was the result of traditions that sprung out of Bronze Age settlements as far back as 1,200 BC (the legendary sacking of Troy), if not much earlier. Similarly, in the New World, the complex empire of the Incas as discovered by Spanish explorers was a slow amalgamation of traditions adopted from Chavin de Huantar, the Moché, the Nazca, and numerous other cultural traditions adjacent to the Andes Mountains and beyond. Thus it stands to reason that the further one delves backward into the earliest forms of human artwork, prior to the creation of complicated belief systems, the more likely one is to find "pure" representative artistic forms. As such, just as with the Moché, their immediate surroundings and the necessities that made daily life possible were what mattered to ancient man first and foremost. Hence the Moché portrayal of fish, corn, and snakes. Hence the Nazca popularity of fruit, lima beans, and birds. Hence the frequent depictions of deer, herd animals, and carnivorous cats in early cave paintings around the globe. These were things important to early cultures. These were things that were either needed for sustenance or dangers that needed avoiding in the precarious world of ages past.

Of course, this is not to say that advanced civilizations emerged concomitantly around the world. In 3,000 BC, ancient Egypt was far more advanced in political structure, religious practice, and in both representative and abstract art form than any known New World counterpart. More relevant to our topic at hand, certainly the Nazca and Moché were far more developed in societal organization than early cave painters who walked the earth thousands of years before them. However, it is curious to note that even with the Moché, a fairly complex society with demonstrable religious and political order, almost all artistic representation is neither abstract nor arbitrary. To put it another way, the Nazca and the Moché had yet to make the artistic shift toward mythological representation that we see in classical Greek, Egyptian, and even Christian art. Furthermore, on a micro-Peruvian level, the artistic style of Nazca artwork, as well as its sociopolitical order, is much simpler than that of the Moché, which lends credence to the supposition that Nazca art, including the infamous Nazca Astronaut, is likely also to be simpler, and so almost entirely representational, which means the "Astronaut" is probably a literal representation of an as of yet unidentified subject.

It is likely that early man had neither the time nor the expendable resources to devote to such speculative activities as creating complex and abstract mythology. At different times around the world, the privilege of mythological, cosmological, and religious supposition came with the confluence of large, like-minded populations. What had early cultures to gain from the exertion of representing such arbitrary figures in ancient art forms? If they had no personal and real connection with such representations, the answer is clearly "nothing." And yet the reality is that ancient man made the conscious decision to depict what we see today as inexplicable, such as the Nazca Astronaut. Such inexplicable artistic representations, created by peoples with less complicated societal structures, and otherwise representational art forms are all around us. As human beings of the Modern Age, we must re-examine each of these critically without resorting to the convenient archaeological methodology of consigning any anomalous artifact or representation to the "mythological" category and ceasing ever to consider it thereafter. Only then will we be able to face up to the full consequences of what they show us.

References
Donnan, Christopher B. *Moche Art of Peru*. Los Angeles: UCLA Latin American Center Publications, 1978.

Cameron Matthew Blount majored in ancient history and classical civilization at UCLA and fueled this passion by studying abroad in Greece and Turkey. Upon completion of a Master's Degree in university administration, one glance at a dissertation was plenty motivation for him to take a post as a university administrator, where he continues to work today.

"THE FRUITFUL MATRIX OF GHOSTS"
THE PSYCHIC INVESTIGATIONS OF SAMUEL TAYLOR COLERIDGE
BY MIKE JAY

"A lady once asked me whether I believed in ghosts and apparitions. I answered with truth and simplicity: No, madam! I have seen far too many myself."

This exchange, recorded by Samuel Taylor Coleridge in 1809, was more than just a chance for a pleasing riposte: it demarcated a subject that had haunted the poet since childhood and to which he would return regularly in both his public and private writings. Typically, the definitive tome that he promised never materialized; yet over many years, in fragments and the occasional sustained burst, Coleridge evolved a psychology of ghosts, visions, and apparitions that was more ambitious than any previously attempted. His interest was not in proving that the supernatural was "real"; rather, he believed that the rational investigation of miraculous events functioned, among other things, as "a weapon against superstition." But he was equally unsatisfied with the debunking spirit that saw all spectral experiences as no more than the errors and weaknesses of the gullible. For him, supernatural-seeming events proved much more: they held the key to understanding the deep mysteries of the imagination, and the powers of the mind to shape reality itself.

His response to the unnamed lady, later published in his journal *The Friend*, had first appeared in a notebook entry dated precisely to midnight on Sunday 12 May 1805. On this occasion he had been dozing at a table in the vast library-cum-saloon of the Treasury in Valetta, Malta, when he had opened his eyes to see a man who wasn't there.

Coleridge had exiled himself to Malta the previous year to break the spell of his opium addiction and failed marriage, and his grand surroundings mirrored the fact that, for the only time in his life, he was holding down a steady and important job: public secretary to the Governor of the island, writing strategic reports on the Mediterranean for the British navy. As usual he had passed a sociable evening among diplomats and civil servants, the last of whom, another secretary named Mr. Dennison, had bid him goodnight ten minutes previously. Coleridge had meant to retire too, but instead had nodded off. When he opened his eyes, he saw Mr. Dennison still sitting across the table from him.

His eyes closed once more, puzzlement mingling with sleep, and when he opened them again he realized that he was in the presence of a waking vision. The Mr. Dennison he had just seen, he now realized, had been a wraith-like illusion, a head and shoulders suspended in mid-air like the grin of the Cheshire cat. The one he saw now was a fully formed simulacrum; yet, as he roused himself to observe it, he became aware that it was somehow less substantial than the man himself. It had a wispy quality, as if seen through thin smoke, or "like a face in a clear stream." As he focused more clearly, the table before it and the library shelves behind became more solidly real, yet the figure maintained a "sort of distinct shape and colour" that gave it a feeling of an illusion superimposed by some kind of optical trickery against its surroundings.

Coleridge reached for his notebook and, "not three minutes having intervened," began to scribble furiously, attempting to record every detail of the apparition while it was still fresh in his mind. As he did so, he began to notice shapes in front of him that were suggestive of the now-vanished illusion. Before him on the table, in the sight-line where the spectral Mr. Dennison had materialized, was a glass flask of port covered in leather; it still had an oddly human shape, and he "clearly detected that this high-shouldered hypochondrical bottle-man had a great share in producing the effect." The chair opposite him, too, was upholstered in leather, with metal studs around its edges that caught the light, picking out another suggestively human shape that framed that of the bottle. As he focused on these details, the illusion began to reform faintly, though this time "I snapped the spell before it had assumed a recognisable form."

But there was more to this business than mere tricks of light, shade, and perspective: Coleridge was keenly aware that a psychological component was also in play. This had been no terrifying specter or vengeful ghost; it had held no more for him than a kind of curiosity and aesthetic fascination. This was surely a product of his own state of mind as he had observed it: he had been "pleased with it as a philosophical case" rather than frightened by it. How differently might the illusion have developed if the hairs on his neck had decided to rise in involuntary dread? And yet, as he considered his state of mind, it occurred to him that "the state of the brain and nerves after distress and agitation" might have played its part, too. Coleridge rarely had to search far to identify a source of nervous malaise, and the evening of 12 May 1805 was no exception: only the previous day he had been badly shaken when three stray dogs had gone for him in the streets of Valetta, one of them sinking its teeth into his left calf. Might his curiously placid vision have been a mental trick triggered by a temporarily forgotten nervous stress, but enacted when he happened to be in a state of contemplative tranquility?

The causes and components of the vision, then, could be sought equally in the external stage-settings and in the inner theatre of the observer's mind. But Coleridge omits another possibility; one that many modern commentators would argue was the most salient of all: opium. Coleridge had not yet reached the point in his life where his narcotic habit was widely known, and it was only when he was posthumously outed by his protégé and fellow-addict Thomas de Quincey that his reputation, and myth, would become inseparable from the drug. But his heavy use of Kendal's Black Drop, his favored, super-strength laudanum tincture, had begun in the Lake District in the winter of 1801, and his attempt to shake free of it in the Mediterranean sunshine had been at best a mixed success. The voyage had begun well, with stimulating views and sea air distracting him from his medication, but storms, sea-sickness, and his cramped cabin had eventually shredded his nerves and reduced him to almost constant dosing: he had felt himself becoming the nightmare-haunted walking corpse of his signature work thus far, *The Rime of the Ancient Mariner.* Arriving in Malta, the change of scene and exotic landscapes had spurred him on to a healthy regime of country walks and clean living; but over the winter he had relapsed once more, alternating days of brisk diplomatic business with nights of furtive indulgence in spirits, narcotics and lurid, luxurious dreams. As he nodded off at the library table at midnight, there is every likelihood that he was dosed to the gills.

Still, the spectral vision of Mr. Dennison before Coleridge's waking eyes is not entirely typical of opium's effects, which tend towards dreamy interior reveries rather than the hallucinatory extrusions into waking reality that are more readily achieved by other psychoactive substances. The drug's psychic hallmarks for Coleridge at this point, to judge by many harrowing notebook entries, were the nightmares that regularly woke him up screaming, sweating, and gasping for breath, with skin-crawling recollections of being pursued, buried alive, mutilated, or infected with hideous diseases. He did not associate these with his opium use, and in fact tended to increase his dose when they occurred in the hope of a sounder sleep; the side-effect of opium that he consciously dreaded most was constipation, with its wrenching gut spasms and the accompanying agony and shame of the only effective remedy, the enema. Yet his periods of exceptionally high opium dosage did produce crawling visual effects at the periphery of his vision: in the latter stages of the voyage to Malta he records faces leering at him from the cloths in his cabin, and flapping sails appearing to him as fish gasping and floundering on the deck. Opium may not be adequate as the sole explanation of Coleridge's vision, but it should probably have been included in his otherwise exhaustive list.

The notebook entry that began in the throes of a vision concluded with a resolution: he would make a similar record whenever such events occurred in the future. "Often and often I have had similar experiences," he wrote, "and therefore resolved to write down the particulars whenever any new instance should occur." He also began to investigate accounts of miracles and other supernatural experiences that he felt might be analogous to his own, and to develop a theory that might account for them.

Then as now, there were essentially two schools of thought, to neither of which he could entirely subscribe. The first was a religious faith that asserted that miracles were the work of God, who permitted the laws of nature to be overridden in special circumstances to contribute to His greater glory. This was a view that had been delicately teased apart by Enlightenment philosophers such as David Hume, whose essay "On Miracles" had argued that since miracles were by definition impossible, there could never be any such thing as sufficient evidence for them. Coleridge had also read the German philosophers such as G.E. Lessing who had gone further, dissecting the transmission of miracles from unknowable first-person testimonies via a process of Chinese whispers to suitably pious and inspirational narratives.

Although never without religious convictions, Coleridge had always taken the rationalists' side against belief in miracles, which represented for him the irrational and obscurantist aspects of a faith that needed to justify its authority to the modern age in rational terms. Yet his debunking zeal was tempered by his voracious curiosity about visionary experience, and perhaps even by a little envy of those who had achieved immortality by bringing their visions into the world. He agreed with the critics who argued that the mystics had mistaken their inner worlds for external divinities, but he did not want to rid the world of miracles: rather, he was searching for ways to include miracles in a novel understanding of it.

For this reason, he was equally dissatisfied with the rational alternative to religious faith. This was the theory, developed by philosophers such as John Locke, that miracles and supernatural experiences were simply errors of cognition, perceptions that had been wrongly associated in the mind and colored by memories, fables, and fancies. For Coleridge this theory gave too little credit to the mind, and too much to a mundane conception of reality. He wanted an explanation that did more than dismiss such experiences as perceptual illusions: one that could explore, as he had with his vision of Mr. Dennison, the active role played by the imagination in their creation. He proceeded, as he often did, to coin a new term to describe such experiences: "supersensual," a rendering perhaps of the German word *übersinnlich*, developed by the mystic Jacob Boehme and included by Goethe in his *Faust*. "Supernatural" was a term that made grand and unjustifiable claims—that we know the laws of nature fully, and that we know the experiences that we designate as miracles and apparitions to be outside their frame. "Supersensual," by contrast, only asserts that these experiences break our laws of perception and consensus reality, without making any judgment about their ultimate status. Some of Coleridge's similar coinages, such as "psychosomatic," have entered the language and are still with us; "supersensual" is one that has not, but perhaps deserves to have done so.

Four years after his notebook entry in Malta, Coleridge made his most sustained attempt to describe this new territory, in a pair of conjoined essays. The first trained his psychological lens on one of the most famous "supernatural" events in the Christian canon; the second, in a classic Coleridgean trajectory, brought the subject back to himself, and his fine-grained self-observation.

The first essay was entitled *Luther's Visions in the Warteburg*, and examined in detail one of the founding myths of Protestantism: that Martin Luther, imprisoned in the Warteburg castle in 1521, had been visited by the Devil while translating the New Testament into German, and had banished him by throwing his inkstand at him. Coleridge himself had visited the castle, towering on its cliff above the town of Eisenach, and had been shown the incorruptible black spot where Luther's ink had hit the wall, and where "the said marvellous blot bids defiance to all the toils of the scrubbing brush, and is to remain a sign for ever." Coleridge was prepared to leave to the reader's judgment "whether the great man did ever throw his inkstand at his Satanic Majesty;" he proposed instead to anatomize Luther's visions in same way that he had his own.

He began, as his self-investigations so often began, in the stomach. Luther was not starving in a dungeon; on the contrary, he was "treated with every kindness," including a much richer diet than he was accustomed to, which "had begun to undermine his former unusually strong health." He recorded "many and most distressing effects of indigestion," with which Coleridge was quick to identify—"the common effect of de-ranged digestion in men of sedentary habits, who are at the same time in-tense thinkers"—and to extrapolate from Luther's unaccustomed luxury to an explanation for him being "plagued with temptations both from the flesh and the devil." The nervous effects of his indigestion would have been most pronounced, as Coleridge's own were, in his "unconscious half-sleeps, or rather those rapid alterations of the sleeping with the half-waking state, which is the true witching time"—or, in a more expressive phrase, "the fruitful matrix of ghosts." In these Luther might, as the au-thor had done in the saloon in Valetta, "have had a full view of the room in which he was sitting," with walls, floor, writing-table, pen, paper and inkstand all clearly perceived, and "at the same time a brain-image of the devil, vivid enough to have acquired apparent outness," superimposed upon the background, its subtly shifting tones and contours suggesting perhaps, to Luther, not illusion but supernatural origin.

This explanation lacks the multifactoral subtlety of Coleridge's dis-section of his own visions, and it seems that some of his readers may have commented as much, as he followed it up with a second piece, apologizing that "the theory of Luther's apparitions [was] stated perhaps too briefly in the preceding essay"—and adding, with a parodic touch of self-pity, that "I will endeavour to make my ghost theory more clear to those of my readers, who are fortunate enough to find it obscure in consequence of their own good health and unshattered nerves." This is the cue for an exquisite description of an optical effect that he used to observe regularly as the winter dusk descended on his study in Keswick, and the fire in his hearth, reflected in his window, began to superimpose itself on the darkening lake and valley outside. The fire emerged as day-light faded, suspended in the distant landscape; as darkness came on, it seemed to grow closer and more dominant, until the arrival of night, when 'the window became a perfect looking-glass; save only that my books on the side shelves of the room were lettered, as it were, on their backs with stars." Here was an optical mechanism for "the phantom from Luther's brain" that might have played into the fruitful matrix of ghosts: the inkstand might, like the port decanter in Malta, have been a hitherto unnoticed foreground detail that nevertheless had "a considerable influ-ence in the production of the fiend, and of the hostile act by which his obtrusive visit was repelled."

To this optical effect must, as ever, be added the state of mind of the observer, and the human readiness to craft meaning from the random. "If we are in anxious expectation," for example, "the babbling of a brook will appear to be the voice of a friend, for whom we are waiting, calling out our own names." These are not simply mechanical errors of perception. They are the products of our minds, which are always working subconsciously to shape the reality around us; supersensual visions are the moments when we catch them up to their constant but otherwise unnoticed tricks. By such increments Coleridge works his way towards the beginnings of a unified theory, the "great law of the imagination," that "a likeness in part tends to become a likeness of the whole:" the brain is always busy recognizing, replicating, expanding, extemporizing, and filling in the gaps. Under the right circumstances, humble decanters and inkstands can morph into human or demonic entities, at which point they may do anything that such entities might be expected to do: walk, speak, wear evening dress, or waggle their pointed tails. Visions are no aberration, but an insight into the ways in which our minds are constantly extrapolating, stitching together a plausible reality from whatever fragments are to hand, in a restless search for patterns that fit the established pigeon-holes of memory and belief.

There is much more that follows from this—nothing less than a new psychology—but, having tantalized himself and the reader, Coleridge announces reluctantly that he is unable to do it justice. "I have long wished to devote an entire work to the subject of dreams, visions, ghosts and witchcraft," he insists, and "I have indeed a memorandum-book filled with records of these phaenomena, many of them interesting as facts and data for psychology, and affording some valuable materials for a theory of perception and its dependence on memory and the imagination." But the death of his collaborator on these theories, the gifted and tragic pottery heir Tom Wedgwood, makes it too painful to pursue—or, perhaps, Coleridge is aware that his insights amount to no more than flashes and fragments that he can stitch together with greater or lesser conviction in his own head, but which he fears will unravel if he attempts to order them and bring them to the page.

Yet if Coleridge abandoned his direct assault on ghosts and visions, his researches nevertheless fed into the restless stream of his theories of the imagination, and particularly its implications for poetry, literature, and drama. "In certain sorts of dreams," he noted, "the dullest wight becomes a Shakespeare." But how can these supersensual effects, created so richly and seamlessly by the mind, be replicated by the writer? He continued to develop the idea that the imagination was not merely a mechanical process, but an organic one, where thoughts and ideas were diffused, recombined, and recreated; his favored analogy became that of a plant, something that develops from a small seed into something far greater than the sum of its parts, transcending the energies that produced it and evolving its own inner life.

These investigations led him to one of his most enduring coinages, the "willing suspension of disbelief," or "suspended state," that poetry or drama must evoke to allow the reader or viewer to believe in characters and scenes that are "supernatural, or at least romantic." This is an effect that is achieved by a mixture of external scene-setting and careful, often subconscious priming of the audience's expectations and imaginations: these conditions, like those that precede waking visions, combine to make the observer receptive to supersensual effects that spill out of reality's habitual confines. Coleridge's "great law of the imagination" was never codified, but neither was it entirely abandoned: it was merely folded into his literary theories, where it vegetated, hybridized and absorbed new sustenance. It emerged as "willing suspension of disbelief," the subliminal compact between subject and object that allows the observer to engage their own imagination, to finesse a middle ground between skepticism and belief, and thus to transform illusion into reality— whether reading *Kubla Khan*, watching *Hamlet*, or calmly observing the apparition of a Mr. Dennison across a library table.

Mike Jay is the author of several books, mostly on the history of drugs and madness, and a longtime contributor to Fortean Times *and* Strange Attractor Journal. *His most recent book,* The Atmosphere of Heaven, *tells the story of the discovery (by Coleridge, among others) of nitrous oxide, or laughing gas. His website is http://mikejay.net*

A Primer for Paranormal Enthusiasts:
Part 1: Magnetic Fields and Haunting Phenomena
Part 2: Temperature in Haunting Experiences
By Bryan Williams, Annalisa Ventola, and Mike Wilson

Part 1: Magnetic Fields And Haunting Phenomena

One need not be a chamber to be haunted,
One need not be a house;
The brain has corridors surpassing
Material place.
— Emily Dickinson, "Ghosts" (circa 1896)

...No one's at the door. You suggest a ghost perhaps a phantom I agree
with this in part. Something is with us I can't put my finger on...
— Tori Amos, "Wednesday" (2002)

Introduction

Reports of haunting phenomena are often characterized by two types of ostensibly anomalous phenomena that may repeatedly occur over long periods of time in a given location. There are subjective phenomena that tend to be experienced by our senses, such as seeing apparitions or ghosts, sensing an unseen presence (sometimes accompanied by feelings of apprehension or fear), and hearing various kinds of sounds that may either be suggestive of physical disruptions (e.g. crashes and banging noises) or be suggestive of a presence (e.g., voices, footsteps, doors opening and shutting). Then there are phenomena that may have some degree of physical objectivity, such as floating lights ("orbs"), temperature variations ("cold spots," which can also be subjective, but may sometimes be measured with a thermometer), electrical disturbances, and the occasional instance of apparent object movement.

One of the goals of haunting research has been to determine whether or not such phenomena may have a rational explanation in terms of the known principles and laws of physics. Parapsychologists often take measurements of the surrounding physical environment in reportedly haunted areas to see if, and how, they may differ from control areas that have had no reports of hauntings. One of the rather consistent findings to emerge from taking such measurements is the indication that haunting occurrences may be associated with magnetic field activity. Additionally, many amateur paranormal enthusiasts have been taking measurements using magnetometers in their attempted efforts to search for spirits in reputedly haunted houses (Coghlan, 1998-1999). Here, we wish to provide a basic primer—a sort of "crash course," if you will—on what parapsychologists have learned about magnetic fields and hauntings, so that their findings may help guide the efforts of paranormal enthusiasts in conducting their investigations.

We give a basic overview of magnetic fields and how they might relate to hauntings based on the current parapsychological literature, and provide some useful tips on what to look out for during field investigations and how to properly interpret findings. This will help make sure that any measurements taken by paranormal enthusiasts are a bit more reliable, better collected, and more soundly interpreted.

We begin with the recognition that there are two main types of magnetic fields that paranormal enthusiasts should be aware of: geomagnetic fields and electromagnetic fields.

Geomagnetism

Geomagnetic fields are DC fields that are produced naturally by the Earth. Although the precise mechanisms have not yet been fully worked out, it is thought that the Earth's magnetic field is largely produced through the fluid motion of the Earth's molten iron core (Buffett, 2000). The circular motion of the core may give rise to electrical currents, which in turn generate a magnetic field [1]. Although the geomagnetic field (GMF) of the Earth averages around 500 milligauss [2], there are a number of things that can produce notable changes in the strength of the GMF in certain areas of the planet. These can include seismic activity along fault zones (Persinger, 1985), electrical activity during thunderstorms, and large amounts of magnetic or electrically conductive minerals present in the surrounding geology of a given area. In addition, increases in cosmic radiation from space, as a result of sunspots, solar flares, and similar stellar phenomena, may sometimes greatly change the

GMF strength as this radiation interacts with the boundary of the GMF in the upper atmosphere (Lyon, 2000), one of the things that can lead to geomagnetic storms.

There has been considerable evidence gathered to suggest that certain forms of human behavior (e.g., sleep disturbances, mood shifts, and increases in anxiety) may coincide with changes in the activity of the geomagnetic field (see Persinger, 1987, for a review of this evidence), suggesting that the GMF may interact in some way with the workings of the brain. Some studies also suggest that people who happen to have particularly sensitive temporal lobes, a condition sometimes brought about through temporal lobe epilepsy or brain injuries, may be more susceptible to changes in GMF activity (e.g., Fuller et al., 1995; Persinger, 2001; Persinger & Koren, 2001, pp. 183-184).

These findings were extended to apparitional experiences when neuroscientist Michael Persinger and his colleagues at Laurentian University in Canada reported findings that suggested that the geomagnetic activity tended to be stronger on days in which people reported seeing apparitions of people that had recently died (Persinger, 1988; Persinger & Schaut, 1988). When extended to haunting cases, strong geomagnetic fields (around 200 milliGauss or more above the average for the Earth's GMF) have been found at reputed haunt sites (Roll & Persinger, 2001, pp. 154-163), which often seems to be related to either the structure of buildings in, or the geology of the area around the haunt site as noted above (for example, some structures contained materials that could potentially harbor magnetic fields, such as stone or mesh wiring; or were built near fault zones).

In attempting to measure geomagnetic fields, one of the simplest and least expensive devices that a paranormal enthusiast can use is the Tri-Field Natural EM Meter, manufactured by Alphalab, Inc. [3]. Rather than measuring the strength of the GMF in the local area, the Natural EM Meter measures the *changes* in the local GMF that may result from one or more of the natural phenomena discussed above. This meter gives readings of these changes in units of microTesla, and a useful conversion factor to note for our purposes is that 1 microTesla = 10 milligauss (Hafemeister, 1996, p. 975). We should note here that since the Natural EM Meter is measuring magnetic changes, it is very sensitive to even the slightest movement of one's hand, and thus the needle can move about erratically and potentially produce a false reading if one is holding it and walking about during an investigation. One way to reduce this is to place the meter on a stationary surface (such as a table) and let the needle to fall to zero before taking any readings.

Electromagnetism

Electromagnetic fields are AC fields that are most often produced artificially by electrical power currents such as those found in our homes. In some instances, they may also be produced naturally by geophysical sources, such electricity produced through seismic pressure on conductive rock along fault zones (Persinger, 1985, 1987), and very low frequency atmospherics, which are electromagnetic pulses produced from electrical discharges after a lightning strike that average around 0.6 milliGauss (Schienle et al., 1998).

The issue of possible health effects in humans due to electromagnetic field (EMF) exposure has received a great deal of attention over the past several decades (Hafemeister, 1996; Portier & Wolfe, 1998; Zipse, 1993), and this may still be a relevant issue today with the large number of computers, electronics, and appliances that have been introduced into the home and workplace. Prolonged exposure to the magnetic fields given off by these devices may provide a reason as to why haunt-related experiences are sometimes reported in new and fairly recent buildings, as opposed to the stereotypical old, abandoned, and eerie-looking building that plays host to urban legends. For example, Persinger, Koren, and O'Connor (2001; Persinger & Koren, 2001, pp. 184-187) investigated reports of haunt phenomena (including apparitions, sensing a presence and an unseen touch, nightmares, breathing & whispering sounds, and light flashes) in the small home of a young adult couple. The house itself contained a large amount of electronics and appliances, and was described as being "overwired" and not properly grounded.

Concern has also been raised over the effects that electromagnetic field exposure may have on brain functioning and resulting mental health (Paneth, 1993; O'Connor, 1993), and at least some experimental studies have seemingly demonstrated an effect. For example, two studies have observed possible changes in brain wave activity on an electroencephalogram (EEG) following brief (2 sec.) exposure to EMFs as strong as 780 milliGauss and higher (Bell et al., 1992; von Klitzing, 1991), similar to the levels we may find at haunt areas. Persinger, Richards, and Koren (1997) found brain wave changes when lower strength magnetic fields (10 milligauss) were applied over longer periods of time (several minutes), with these changes even continuing for a short time after the magnetic field has been removed. A review of experimental studies also suggests that changes in brain chemistry and hormone levels may sometimes occur in response to EMF exposure (Reiter, 1993). A considerable amount of evidence suggests that EMF exposure can also affect sleep (Sher, 2000), which might contribute to haunt experiences that occur during sleeping hours. Gangi and Johansson (2000) have even proposed a model which suggests that EMF exposure may cause certain skin cells to release certain inflammatory substances that may cause itching and other skin sensations. If their model is correct, it may perhaps be a way to account for some of the strange skin and touching sensations that people sometimes experience at haunt areas.

The suggestion that electromagnetic field exposure might be tied in some way to apparitional experiences comes from both laboratory studies and field investigations. In the laboratory, Persinger, Tiller, and Koren (2000) were able to study the experiences of a man who had reported haunt phenomena in his home a few years before. When a 10 milligauss EMF with a complex wave pattern was applied to his brain, the man reported experiencing brief "rushes of fear" and various odd sensations, followed by him seeing a visual image that seemed to resemble the apparition he saw in his home. Changes in the man's brain wave activity were also observed by EEG in conjunction with his experience. See also Persinger (2001) and Persinger and Koren (2001, pp. 190-192) for other discussions of this and a related study.

The electromagnetic fields in most buildings tend to average between 0.2 and 2 milligauss. However, various field investigations have found EMFs notably above this average at haunt sites (e.g., Persinger et al., 2001; Roll et al., 1996; Roll & Persinger, 2001, pp. 154-163; Wiseman et al., 2002). This is not always the case, however; there are at least two field investigations that did not find strong EMFs at the haunt sites when measuring for them (Maher, 2000; Maher & Hansen, 1997).

To measure electromagnetic fields, one of the least expensive yet effective devices that a paranormal enthusiast may commonly use is a second type of meter made by Alphalab, the Tri-Field Broadband Meter [4]. This meter is calibrated to measure EMFs such as those generated by power lines, and gives readings in units of milligauss. When taking readings with this meter, it is important to note any possible sources around the meter (e.g., electronics and appliances, power generators, running cars, & electrical wiring) that may naturally cause the meter's needle to move higher or even spike, and which may lead to a false reading.

Comments & Tips on Magnetic Fields at Haunt Areas

We now present some additional comments, as well as some useful tips for paranormal enthusiasts, on the measurement of magnetic fields—both geomagnetic and electromagnetic—at haunt areas during field investigations.

1.) Always take note of the area around the spot you are measuring to make sure that there are no electronics, appliances, power lines or generators, and wiring nearby that may be a natural cause for any magnetic fields you detect. This will enable you to decide if you are getting an anomalous reading, rather than a false one. It is vitally important to recognize that although it appears that magnetic fields may be tied in some way to apparitions and haunting phenomena, *this does not necessarily mean that the presence of fields at haunt areas are due to ghosts.* Many less-experienced investigators have immediately jumped to this conclusion, and one can see that it is generally not correct when one realizes that there are many sources in non-haunted locations that can generate these fields by conventional means. These same sources may also be found at haunt sites.

2.) Be sure to take baseline readings of the haunt site to determine the average magnetic field strength of the site. It can be helpful to compare readings taken from haunt areas where ghostly phenomena has been reported with readings taken from nearby areas where no phenomena has been reported ("control" areas). It is useful to establish a baseline magnetic reading that can be compared to the magnetic field readings at the haunt area, which may help determine just how different the two are from each other (a basic indication of how "anomalous" the magnetic fields in the haunt area are). Measurements should first be recorded throughout the haunt site to determine the average magnetic field strength of the site, as well as locate any areas where there might be natural irregularities in the field due to power generators, power lines entering the building, and/or a large amount of electronics, appliances, or electrical wiring gathered in one room. This practice will also help in accomplishing the goal in Tip #1.

Houran and Brugger (2000) have suggested that measurements at haunt areas should also be compared to those taken in a "control" area where no haunting phenomena have been reported. This can help to establish that the measurements from haunt areas are anomalous, and not just part of the regular background fields of the area. As noted above, there are several conventional sources at non-haunt sites that may produce large magnetic fields from time-to-time, and some of these same sources may also be found in haunt sites. If the measurements from the haunt area and the control area are close to each other in strength when they are compared, then this may hint at these conventional sources being involved, and the readings at the haunt area not being particularly anomalous.

3.) Investigators may want to try to detect changes in the magnetic field over time by taking repeated measurements in different areas of a room, and/or different areas of the haunt site to see if there is any potential sign of a gradual increase or decrease across the haunt site. A number of field investigations reported in the parapsychological literature are beginning to indicate that it is not the absolute strength or intensity of the magnetic field at the haunt site that may be important, but rather the way that the field changes over time. In at least two of the haunts investigated by noted parapsychologist William Roll (reported in Roll & Persinger, pp. 156-157), the strength of the magnetic fields were noted to either be gradually increasing or decreasing as one moved from one side of the haunt site to the other, suggesting that the field was changing throughout the site. In the course of investigating haunt reports at Hampton Court Palace in England, Wiseman et al. (2002, 2003) noted in a statistical comparison that the magnetic field changes in areas of the palace where haunting phenomena had been reported were significantly different from the field changes in areas where no phenomena were reported. They also found in another statistical comparison that the number of unusual experiences reported by tourists visiting the Palace was also related in some way to the magnetic field changes at the site. Braithwaite and associates have taken several measurements in a specific bedroom at Muncaster Castle in England (Braithwaite, 2004; Braithwaite et al., 2004). People sleeping in the bed found in that bedroom have reported hearing voices at night that sound like children crying, and measurements were taken in the area around the pillow of the bed and later compared to control measurements taken towards the center of the room, where the voices apparently came from. Notable changes in magnetic field strength were noted over this very short distance (roughly a few meters), suggesting sharp magnetic field changes across the space of a single room. Most recently, Terhune et al. (2007) found suggestive differences when statistically comparing the magnetic field changes in areas where haunt phenomena were reported to control areas where no phenomena occurred. Similarly, the magnetic fields applied to the brain that Persinger and his associates use to simulate haunt-related experiences (Persinger, 2001;

Persinger & Koren, 2001; Persinger et al., 2000) are often composed of complex patterns that can change the structure of the fields.

4.) Carefully log all magnetic readings and conditions, including specific locations where readings were taken, time that readings were taken, and the length of time that the magnetic field was present. If floor plans of the site(s) under investigation are available, use copies of these to record your readings. Otherwise, it might be beneficial to draft your own floor plan of the site(s), time and resources permitting. If one hopes to have their results taken seriously, it is often better to have a complete record or log of the investigation, particularly of all measurements made. Human memory alone is too unreliable because it is subject to bias and error. Having a record may also help to reveal possible patterns in the activity at the haunt site that may hint at a possible natural source for it (e.g., some EMFs in homes and buildings may sometimes change at regular intervals when certain equipment or appliances, such as air conditioners, refrigerators, etc., turn on and off).

Although it is not meant to be comprehensive, we hope that this primer provides a starting basis for those paranormal enthusiasts who wish to take their approach to haunting investigations a step further.

PART 2: TEMPERATURE IN HAUNTING EXPERIENCES

Introduction

Among the various kinds of subjective perceptual experiences that one may report having in a reputedly haunted house, one of the most common may be sensing a noticeable change (typically a drop) in the ambient background temperature within the space of a room (Coghlan, 1998-1999; Osis, 1982; Roll & Persinger, 2001; Roll et al., 1996; Turner, 1970). These apparent "cold spots" may occur spontaneously and only be a fleeting feeling, or they may be persistent over time, seeming to be a characteristic part of the haunted locale and perhaps adding to its mystique.

In a related manner, some sightings of apparitions or ghosts have been accompanied by sudden feelings of cold. In his classic book *Apparitions*, psychical researcher G. N. M. Tyrrell (1953/1961) had noticed a fair degree of consistency across the reports of witnesses who had such feelings, with some stating that it was like, "...a jug of cold water poured on the nape of my neck," or "...as if the blood was like ice in my veins," or "...a cold, shivering feeling came over me" (p. 73). Other witnesses gave statements suggesting that the cold sensation had emanated from the apparition itself: "As the figure passed we distinctly felt a cold air," or "Her kiss was like a waft of cold air upon my cheek" (p. 73).

A good illustrative example within the annals of psychical research of how cold sensations play into apparitional and haunting phenomena can be found in the "Morton Ghost" case, documented and reported by[1] nineteen-year-old medical student Rosina C. Despard (Morton, 1892). From about 1882 to 1889, the Despard family repeatedly saw the apparition of a woman dressed in a widow's outfit[2] that would wander through their house in a specific, repetitive pattern. Some of the family also occasionally heard footsteps, and on one such occasion, the footsteps seemed to be pacing up and down the second-floor landing. This drew the attention of Rosina's three sisters and two family maids, who emerged from their rooms with lit candles in their hands to see who was causing the ruckus. As the unseen footsteps passed them, they reported feeling "'a cold wind,' though their candles were not blown out" (p. 320). This suggests that the wind may have been a subjective feeling, and not a physical breeze. On another occasion, when Rosina's sister Edith, her mother, and a maid heard footsteps pass close by them on the landing, they suddenly felt an "icy shiver" (p. 325). Edith herself had an encounter with the spectral widow on another night, while she was singing in the drawing room. She stopped in the middle of her song when she suddenly "...felt a cold, icy shiver, and I saw the figure bend over me, as if to turn over the pages of my song" (p. 325).

Are all such cold sensations during apparitional and haunting phenomena purely in the mind of the witnesses (as the candle example in the Morton case suggests), or do some have an actual physical basis in the environment? To find out, some parapsychologists have taken temperature measurements during field investigations of haunted locations to see if they differ much from control locations where no ghosts or haunt phenomena have been reported. In a similar fashion, many amateur paranormal enthusiasts have taken readings with thermometers as part of their attempts to search for spirits in ostensibly haunted locations (Coghlan, 1998-1999).

We give a brief overview of what parapsychologists have learned so far about temperature in relation to haunting experiences, and provide some useful tips on how to properly collect and interpret temperature readings during field investigations.

Temperature: The Parapsychological Perspective

A glance at the research literature suggests that parapsychologists have gotten a mixed bag of results when taking temperature measurements during field investigations of haunted sites. An initial effort to collect detailed measurements was made in mid-1968 by the Doncaster Group for Psychical Study as part of an investigation of a haunted house in the mining village of Askern, South Yorkshire, England (Turner, 1970). Residents and visitors of the home had reported hearing metallic clicks and other unusual sounds, seeing spectral human figures, and feeling sensations of cold in the living room and bedroom of the home. The cold feelings would even sometimes occur in the living room while it was being warmed by an active fireplace. To objectively explore the cold feelings, the Doncaster Group had set up an array of thermometers in the living room and bedroom, which were monitored during seven separate overnight surveillance sessions. While some of the cold sensations felt by the group were not accompanied by thermal changes and may have been purely subjective, others had produced patterns of potential interest. Cold sensations had occurred at around the same time (between 12:30 and 1:00 A.M.) on four of six surveillance nights, with three of the four occurring in the bedroom (p. 341). When the cold sensations did actually coincide with a marked change in the thermometer readings, the change was a drop of about nine to ten degrees Fahrenheit (p. 352). Some of the thermal changes also coincided with the reported clicking sounds, which the Doncaster Group suspected may have resulted from thermal contraction of the metal building materials in the home (i.e., they may have been the sounds of the house settling with temperature shifts, and may not have been anomalous).

Measures of temperature and humidity were also taken during an extensive field study of an allegedly haunted Illinois home by researchers Devin Terhune, Annalisa Ventola, and James Houran (2007). Apparitions, object movements, and sensed presences were experienced by the residents and a visitor of the home, and the residents' dog was noted to display unusual behaviors at times. When digital temperature and humidity readings collected in the allegedly haunted home were compared to the readings taken in a control home located next-door where no haunt phenomena had been reported, the haunted home was found to be significantly cooler and moister than the control home. However, the three areas within the haunted home where the haunt phenomena were most active did not differ much from four other areas that were less active.

Not all field investigations have found that the background temperature of haunted sites is associated with anomalous experiences, however. In the early part of 2001, researchers from the University of Hertfordshire in England and the University of Edinburgh in Scotland had conducted a field investigation, led by psychologist Richard Wiseman, of the reputedly haunted South Bridge Vaults in Edinburgh. The vaults consist of a series of chambers connected by corridors that were built in the late 18th century to house the poor during the construction of the South Bridge. Poor living conditions and overcrowding had turned the vault area into a disease-ridden slum, and it was abandoned in the 19th century. It was opened again to the public in 1996 for tours, and several tourists and guides have reported seeing apparitions, hearing footsteps, and sensing an unseen presence in the vaults since that time. To explore the reported haunt reports, the researchers monitored several physical variables, including air temperature. Although nearly half of the people (44%) visiting the vaults during the study had reported a haunt-related experience (some of which included sensing a change in temperature), the temperature level and the speed of the air inside the vaults were not significantly related to the amount of experiences people had. Instead, they were more related to the height and amount of lighting in the vaults (Wiseman et al., 2003), suggesting that haunt experiences can have more than one cause.

To explore the role that temperature might play in ghost experiences, Dean Radin and Jannine Rebman (1996) had monitored the temperature (among other physical variables) inside a custom-built psychomanteum in their laboratory. A psychomanteum is a dark chamber modeled after an ancient Greek oracle that is used as way to artificially induce apparitional experiences through the ages-old technique of scrying (i.e., gazing into a reflective surface; in this case, a mirror). As volunteers sat inside the psychomanteum chamber and attempted to have an apparitional experience, Radin and Rebman monitored certain aspects of their physiology (e.g., their heart rate, skin resistance, and blood-pulse volume) to see if these might be associated with changes in the environment during an apparitional experience. The results of the study indicated that shifts in the volunteers' physiology were most often associated with changes in air temperature inside the psychomanteum, although not all of these may have been related to experiences of apparitions. While preparing for the psychomanteum session, three people (the experimenter, the session facilitator, and the volunteer) were all in the chamber at the same time, which may have brought about an increase in air temperature due to their body heat. The temperature would have begun to drop soon after the volunteer was left alone in the chamber, and this could have coincided with shifts in the volunteers' physiology as they begun to relax. Thus, some of the temperature changes seen in this study might have had a natural cause. A closer study of psychomanteum temperature changes in relation to apparitional experiences is currently being conducted by researchers at Liverpool Hope University in England (Parsons & O'Keeffe, 2006).

The results of these parapsychological studies suggest that temperature changes may play a part in some, but probably not all, haunting experiences. Some of these changes may be purely subjective, but others may have a physical basis that is measurable using thermometers and other kinds of thermal sensors.

The Peltier Effect: A Natural Source for "Cold Spots?"

If some "cold spots" found in haunt sites are indeed physical occurrences, then could there be a way to explain their origin? Canadian neuroscientist Michael Persinger (1974, pp. 179-183) thinks that there may indeed a way, one that has its basis in the natural geophysical processes of the Earth. It's called the Peltier effect, and it's rather easy to demonstrate in a physics lab.

Here's a basic overview of how it works: Below ground, there are several layers of mineral and rock that are composed of silicates, which are capable of conducting electricity. Some silicates, such as manganese silicate, are thermoelectric materials that can change temperature when an electrical current is passed through them. Under the right conditions, high voltage electric fields can build up in underground rock layers, either from seismic activity near fault zones, or from electrical activity during thunderstorms (Persinger, 1974, 1985). If enough electrical charge builds up between two rock separate layers of opposite polarity, an electrical current can begin to flow between them. If a slab of thermoelectric material happens to lie in between these two rock layers, the current going through the slab will induce a thermal change, which in most cases would be a decrease. Homes that have been built above these rock layers would then experience a notable drop in temperature as one gets closer in proximity to the layers (this means that they would probably be felt most often in basements or low ground floors). In addition, since the flow of the electrical current between the rock layers would produce a magnetic field, it might be possible to observe a change in magnetic field strength (as measured by a magnetometer; see our previous paper) in conjunction with a sudden drop in the surrounding temperature at a haunt site.

An example of the Peltier effect in action may be found in the case of the White Ranch haunting, investigated in the mid-1990s by noted parapsychologist William Roll of the University of West Georgia (Roll et al., 1996). The case focuses around a Texas hunting lodge built in the 1950s that was renovated by a group of local cowboys. While staying overnight at the lodge, the cowboys would hear various sounds that would often wake them up at night, including what they described as heavy footsteps, loud crashes, and thunderous poundings on the wall. When rising to determine what had caused the noises, they were regularly baffled to find that nothing had fallen or moved, and that there would be no obvious sources for them. Another interesting feature of these noises is that not everyone heard them each time; some of the cowboys stated that they would be awakened by the loudness of the sounds, but then be surprised to find that others in the lodge had slept right through the ruckus. Most relevant to our discussion, the cowboys would also report feeling sharp drops in temperature in their rooms at night; one cowboy had described it as being "as cold as ice," causing him to shiver underneath the bedsheets.

The subsequent field investigation of the lodge by Roll and his assistant Lisa Sheehan did indeed reveal that the drops in temperature at night were coincident with notable, short-lived increases in the environmental magnetic fields occurring in the early morning hours. (Lisa also reported feeling the sharp temperature drop while staying in one of the lodge rooms.) The lodge itself was situated close to a fault zone, and seismic occurrences in this fault may have generated high electrical and magnetic activity. In addition to contributing to the Peltier effect, the effects of this activity on the brains of people may have produced auditory hallucinations, leading them to hear the loud noises in their mind that would not be heard by others.

In some cases, the Peltier effect may even produce the opposite effect—intense heating—when the direction of the electrical current is reversed. Such an effect may have been seen in another haunt case investigated by Roll in Indiana (Roll & Persinger, 2001, pp. 153-154). Aside from seeing apparitions, hearing unusual sounds, smelling foul and flowery scents, and experiencing cold spots in various areas of their home, the family in the case also occasionally reported fires that would spontaneously erupt and scorch their ceiling, which were not due to electrical sparks or other common causes. Roll noticed that the home was situated within a triangular-shaped area of high-tension power lines that may have produced strong electromagnetic fields, and that there an underground stream beneath the home that may have helped generate a high geomagnetic field. Both of these could have perhaps contributed to Peltier effects that spontaneously shifted in current direction.

Tips on Temperature in Haunt Areas

We now present some useful tips for paranormal enthusiasts on taking temperature readings during field investigations of haunts. Several of these tips can be used in conjunction with those we offered in our previous primer on magnetic fields.

1.) *Always* take note of the area you are measuring to make sure that any notable changes in temperature that you pick up are not due to natural causes, such as air conditioners or heaters, open ventilation ducts, wall cracks, or weather changes. This will better ensure that the change you are getting is more likely to be an anomalous one, rather than a false one. Although this tip is pretty much common sense, it is also perhaps the most important one to follow. The difficult thing about using temperature as a variable to monitor for the occurrence of haunt phenomena is that it can have so many natural and artificial sources. The closer you pay attention to your surroundings and remain aware, the better the chance you have of ruling out conventional sources. As you begin to do this, the possibility that you are getting something anomalous, and thus something more interesting, begins to go up. Be sure to note down any conventional sources that you may in your investigation log or report. Also, for outdoor haunt sites, be sure to note down the general weather conditions (e.g., cloud cover, presence of wind, etc.) throughout the period of the field investigation, and it might be a good idea to check the local weather reports on TV or in the newspaper prior to the investigation. The more observant and careful you are, the more seriously others will consider your findings.

2.) Be sure to take baseline temperature readings of the haunt site in order to determine how cold (or even warm) the site initially is. It can be helpful to compare readings taken from haunt areas where ghostly phenomena has been reported with readings taken from nearby areas where no phenomena has been reported ("control" areas). This is one basic way to test whether or not haunt sites may be colder (or even warmer) than ordinary sites. Once you have a baseline established, you can compare it to other readings taken at a later time to determine whether or not a temperature change has indeed occurred over time, particularly if a haunt occurrence happens to take place. Measurements should first be recorded throughout the haunt site to determine the average background temperature of the site, as well as locate any areas where there might be sources that could naturally produce a change. If you have a floor plan of the haunt site available, you might note down the readings on it, along with the locations of ventilation ducts, air conditioners and heaters, windows, and other sources where air might leak into the site. This practice will also help in accomplishing the goal in Tip #1. Houran and Brugger (2000) have suggested that measurements at haunt areas should also be compared to those taken in a "control" area where no haunting phenomena have been reported. This can help to establish that the readings taken from haunt areas are anomalous, and not just part of the regular background atmosphere of the area. Field studies by parapsychologists have produced some results to suggest that haunt sites may be colder than control sites (e.g., Terhune et al., 2007), but more data on this is needed to further and better test this hypothesis. Paranormal enthusiasts can be a major help in doing this. Also, *always* be sure to note your units of measure (i.e., Celsius or Fahrenheit) for both accuracy and clarity.

3.) **To improve accuracy in temperature readings during the investigation, you might invest in a good digital thermometer.** While standard mercury bulb thermometers can certainly be useful in field investigations to take general background readings at haunt sites, the late parapsychologist Karlis Osis (1982) once observed that these thermometers may be too slow and crude to detect any fleeting changes in temperature that may result from haunt phenomena. Today's digital thermometers are capable of registering such slight changes in real-time temperature with a fairly good amount of accuracy, and thus they may be a bit more reliable and resourceful. A good digital thermometer that is relatively inexpensive (and which also measures humidity) is the Model 63-1032 Indoor/Outdoor Thermometer with Hygrometer, made by Radio Shack. Non-contact infrared thermometers, such as the hand-held Raynger series made by Raytek (http://www.raytek.com), also allow temperature to be monitored accurately and at a slight distance; they are most useful for wide-open spaces, but also tend to be quite expensive ($150+ range). Thermovision cameras and lenses, which visually display temperature fields in an array of false colors (Andrews, 1977), have also recently become relatively inexpensive with improving technology, and can be used for monitoring temperature changes within the space of a room. Some portable ones are made by FLIR Systems, Inc. (http://

www.goinfrared.com/cameras/), but they may still be a bit on the pricey side for most paranormal enthusiasts ($700+).

4.) Consider taking magnetic field readings alongside temperature readings to see if any changes in temperature are accompanied by changes in magnetic field strength, as would be predicted by the Peltier effect. Although the Peltier effect is a plausible mechanism for cold spots in haunt sites, additional data are needed to further test its validity. Again, paranormal enthusiasts can be of help in accomplishing this. While collecting and noting down temperature readings, other members of your group might also collect and note down magnetic field readings in your vicinity. Since most fields produced by the Earth are DC magnetic fields, it is recommended that the Tri-Field Natural EM Meter (the one with the blue label) be used to take magnetic readings (especially since this meter registers *changes* in the local geomagnetic field, which may result from an electrical current as in the Peltier effect). However, some seismic phenomena may also sometimes produce AC electromagnetic fields, so taking readings with the Tri-Field Broadband Meter (the one with the tan label) should also be done from time-to-time. (If possible, you might have members of your group take readings from both meters while you take temperature readings, since the two meters measure different kinds of magnetic fields; one meter may detect a field change that the other is unable to.)

As a basic way to look for a possible relationship between temperature and magnetic field strength, you might consider plotting each set of readings (one for temperature, one for magnetic field) in a line graph drawn on a piece of graph paper, and then compare the two graphs to see if they show any similar patterns (such as both showing a sharp increase, or "spike," at a certain time) with each other. Just as a picture is worth a thousand words, a basic line graph of your data can say a lot about the trends occurring over time at a haunt site.

Conclusion

Although this primer is not meant to be comprehensive, we hope that it will be helpful for paranormal enthusiasts when it comes to measuring temperature, and that it will serve as yet another stepping stone for those who wish to take their approach to haunting investigations a step further.

Acknowledgements

Reproduced with permission from Publicparapsychology.org

Part 1 Notes

1. To get a bit technical, this would follow from Ampere's law (with Maxwell's correction), one of Maxwell's laws that relates electricity to magnetism; see, e.g., Griffiths (1999, p. 323).
2. Magnetic fields are usually measured in one of three main scaled units: Gauss, Tesla, and Gamma. Since many commercial magnetometers often used by paranormal enthusiasts, such as the Broadband Tri-Field Meter made by Alphalab, Inc. (see also Note #3), tend to give magnetic field readings in terms of milliGauss (i.e., one-one thousandth of a Gauss), we will use this unit as our reference point throughout this primer.
3. The Tri-Field Natural EM Meter is similar in appearance to the Tri-Field Broadband Meter (also made by Alphalab), which paranormal enthusiasts also commonly use in investigations, but is recognized by its blue colored label surrounding the dial switch, and by the small knob on the side of the meter. Both types of meters can be purchased from Alphalab http://www.trifield.com).
4. The Tri-Field Broadband Meter is distinguished from the Tri-Field Natural EM Meter by its tan-colored label surrounding the dial switch, and lack of small knob.

Part 2 Notes

1. For reasons of anonymity, Rosina Despard had reported the case under the pseudonym "Miss R. C. Morton," hence its name. Since the house at the center of the case was located in Cheltenham, England, it also came to known by some as the "Cheltenham Ghost" case. The details of the case were independently verified by the prominent psychical researcher Frederic W. H. Myers, who stated that, with one minor exception (an elderly man couldn't recall one event that had happened six years before), he "...found no discrepancy in the independent testimonies" (Morton, 1892, p. 311). Incidentally, Rosina Despard went on to become a practicing physician in forensic medicine, which was quite an achievement for a woman in the 1880s.
2. The Morton ghost's pattern of movement would begin on the second floor of the Despard home, usually after Rosina would hear someone at her bedroom door. Upon opening it, she would see the ghostly widow walking down the landing hallway towards the stairs. The figure would then descend to the ground floor and enter the drawing room, standing at the window on the far side for a time. Then it would exit the room and head for a passage leading to the garden, where it would regularly vanish. On rare occasions, when other people or objects were in its way, the apparition would either simply pass through them, or would make slight deviations in its path to avoid them (Morton, 1892, p. 317, 321). Attempts by Rosina to corner the

apparition were unsuccessful, as it would simply disappear (p. 322). Although it initially appeared "...so solid and life-like that it was often mistaken for a real person," according to Rosina (p. 321), the spectral widow seemed to gradually fade with time, and had completely vanished by 1889. Inquiries by the Despard family suggested that the apparition may have represented the second wife of a previous occupant of the house.

3. One surveillance session showed a steady temperature throughout the night.

4. To add a bit of chemistry for the technically minded, the element silicon in its pure solid, crystallized form is not very electrically conductive. However, when tiny amounts (as small as 0.0001%) of other elements such as arsenic or boron are mixed in; the conductivity of silicon increases greatly, making it a useful component in semiconductor devices (Masterton & Hurley, 1997, pp. 264-265). When combined with oxygen, silicon forms a chemical compound known as silicate ($SiO4$), which can be bonded with other metals. More than 90% of the rocks and minerals found in the Earth's crust are silicate-based materials (Hill & Kolb, 1995, pp. 313-322).

5. Certain mineral crystals, when subjected to intense pressure such as that generated by seismic activity, can produce a certain kind of natural electricity, known as piezoelectricity (see Persinger, 1974, Ch. 5, for more info.).

6. In physics, this would follow from Ampere's law (with Maxwell's correction), one of Maxwell's laws that relates electricity to magnetism (see Griffiths, 1999, p. 323; and Halliday, Resnick, & Walker, 1997, Ch. 30).

7. This case was profiled in a segment of the TV show "Unsolved Mysteries"; a video clip of this segment can be found on YouTube at: http://www.youtube.com/watch?v=8xks0itnI_Y Fahrenheit is most commonly used temperature unit in the United States, and is related to Celsius by the equation $F = (9/5)*C + 32$ degrees, where C is the temperature in Celsius (Halliday, Resnick, & Walker, 1997, p. 457).

Part 1 References

Bell, G. B., Marino, A. A., & Chesson, A. L. (1992). Alterations in brain electrical activity caused by magnetic fields: Detecting the detection process. *Electroencephalography and Clinical Neurophysiology, 83*, 389-397.

Buffett, B. A. (2000). Earth's core and the geodynamo. *Science, 288*, 2007-2012.

Braithwaite, J. J. (2004). Magnetic variances associated with 'haunt-type' experiences: A comparison using time-synchronized baseline measurements. *European Journal of Parapsychology, 19*, 3-28.

Braithwaite, J. J., Perez-Aquino, K., & Townsend, M. (2004). In search of magnetic anomalies associated with haunt-type experiences: Pulses and patterns in dual time-synchronized measurements. *Journal of Parapsychology, 68*, 255-288.

Coghlan, A. (1998—1999). Midnight watch. *New Scientist, 160*, 42—45.

Fuller, M., Dobson, J., Wieser, H. G., & Moser, S. (1995). On the sensitivity of the human brain to magnetic fields: Evocation of epileptiform activity. *Brain Research Bulletin*, 36, 155-159.

Gangi, S., & Johansson, O. (2000). A theoretical model based upon mast cells and histamine to explain the recently proclaimed sensitivity to electric and/ or magnetic fields in humans. *Medical Hypotheses*, 54, 663-671.

Griffiths, D. J. (1999). *Introduction to Electrodynamics* (3rd Ed.). Upper Saddle River, NJ: Prentice-Hall.

Hafemeister, D. (1996). Resource letter BELFEF-1: Biological effects of low-frequency electromagnetic fields. *American Journal of Physics*, 64, 974-981.

Houran, J., & Brugger, P. (2000). The need for independent control sites: A methodological suggestion with special reference to haunting and poltergeist field research. *European Journal of Parapsychology*, 15, 30-45.

Lyon, J. G. (2000). The solar wind-magnetosphere-ionosphere system. *Science*, 288, 1987-1991.

Maher, M. C. (2000). Quantitative investigation of the General Wayne Inn. *Journal of Parapsychology*, 64, 365-390.

Maher, M. C., & Hansen, G. P. (1997). Quantitative investigation of a legally disputed "haunted house." *Proceedings of Presented Papers: The Parapsychological Association 40th Annual Convention* (pp. 184—201). Durham, NC: Parapsychological Association, Inc.

O'Connor, M. E. (1993). Psychological studies in nonionizing electromagnetic energy research. *Journal of General Psychology*, 120, 33-47.

Paneth, N. (1993). Neurobehavioral effects of power-frequency electromagnetic fields. *Environmental Health Perspectives Supplements*, 101, 101-106.

Persinger, M. A. (1985). Geophysical variables and behavior: XXII. The tectonogenic strain continuum of unusual events. *Perceptual and Motor Skills*, 60, 59-65.

Persinger, M. A. (1987). Geopsychology and geopsychopathology: Mental processes and disorders associated with geochemical and geophysical factors. *Experientia*, 43, 92-103.

Persinger, M. A. (1988). Increased geomagnetic activity and the occurrence of bereavement hallucinations: Evidence for melatonin-mediated microseizuring in the temporal lobe? *Neuroscience Letters*, 88, 271-274.

Persinger, M. A. (2001). The neuropsychiatry of paranormal experiences. *Journal of Neuropsychiatry and the Clinical Neurosciences*, 13, 515-524.

Persinger, M. A., & Koren, S. A. (2001). Predicting the characteristics of haunt phenomena from geomagnetic factors and brain sensitivity: Evidence from field and experimental studies. In J. Houran & R. Lange (Eds.) *Hauntings and Poltergeists: Multidisciplinary Perspectives* (pp. 179-194). Jefferson, NC: McFarland & Company, Inc.

Persinger, M. A., Koren, S. A., & O'Connor, R. P. (2001). Geophysical variables and behavior: CIV. Power frequency magnetic field transients (5 microTesla) and reports of haunt experiences within an electronically dense house.

Perceptual and Motor Skills, 92, 673-674.

Persinger, M. A., Richards, P. M., & Koren, S. A. (1997). Differential entrainment of electroencephalographic activity by weak complex electromagnetic fields. *Perceptual and Motor Skills*, 84, 527-536.

Persinger, M. A., & Schaut, G. B. (1988). Geomagnetic factors in subjective telepathic, precognitive, and postmortem experiences. *Journal of the American Society for Psychical Research*, 82, 217-235.

Persinger, M. A., Tiller, S. G., & Koren, S. A. (2000). Experimental simulation of a haunt experience and elicitation of paroxysmal electroencephalographic activity by transcerebral complex magnetic fields: Induction of a synthetic "ghost"? *Perceptual and Motor Skills*, 90, 659-674.

Portier, C. J., & Wolfe, M. S. (Eds.) (1998). *Assessment of Health Effects from Exposure to Power-Line Frequency Electric and Magnetic Fields: NIEHS Working Group Report*. Research Triangle Park, NC: National Institute of Environmental Health Sciences/National Institutes of Health.

Reiter, R. J. (1993). A review of neuroendocrine and neurochemical changes associated with static and extremely low frequency electromagnetic field exposure. *Integrative Physiological and Behavioral Science*, 28, 57-75.

Roll, W. G., Maher, M. C., & Brown, B. (1996). An investigation of reported haunting occurrences in a Japanese restaurant in Georgia. In E. W. Cook (Ed.) *Research in Parapsychology 1992* (pp. 62-67). Lanham, MD: Scarecrow Press.

Roll, W. G., & Persinger, M. A. (2001). Investigations of poltergeists and haunts: A review and interpretation. In J. Houran & R. Lange (Eds.) *Hauntings and Poltergeists: Multidisciplinary Perspectives* (pp. 123-163). Jefferson, NC: McFarland & Company, Inc.

Schienle, A., Stark, R., & Vaitl, D. (1998). Biological effects of very low frequency (VLF) atmospherics in humans: A review. *Journal of Scientific Exploration*, 12, 455-468.

Sher, L. (2000). The effects of natural and man-made electromagnetic fields on mood and behavior: The role of sleep disturbances. *Medical Hypotheses*, 54, 630-633.

Terhune, D. B., Ventola, A., & Houran, J. (2007). An analysis of contextual variables and the incidence of photographic anomalies at an alleged haunt and a control site. *Journal of Scientific Exploration*, 21, 99-120.

von Klitzing, L. (1991). A new encephalomagnetic effect in human brain generated by static magnetic fields. *Brain Research*, 540, 295-296.

Wiseman, R., Watt, C., Greening, E., Stevens, P., & O'Keeffe, C. (2002). An investigation into the alleged haunting of Hampton Court Palace: Psychological variables and magnetic fields. *Journal of Parapsychology*, 66, 387-408.

Wiseman, R., Watt, C., Stevens, P., Greening, E., & O'Keeffe, C. (2003). An investigation into alleged 'hauntings.' *British Journal of Psychology*, 94, 195-211.

Zipse, D. W. (1993). Health effects of extremely low-frequency (50- and 60-Hz) electric and magnetic fields. *IEEE Transactions on Industry Applications*, 29, 447-458.

Part 2 References

Andrews, A. K. (1977). The use of instrumentation to detect temperature fields in haunting, poltergeist, and experimental PK investigations. *Journal of the American Society for Psychical Research, 71,* 333-334.

Coghlan, A. (1998—1999). Midnight Watch. *New Scientist, 160,* 42-45.

Griffiths, D. J. (1999). *Introduction to Electrodynamics* (3rd Ed.). Upper Saddle River, NJ: Prentice-Hall.

Halliday, D., Resnick, R., & Walker, J. (1997). *Fundamentals of Physics* (5th Ed.). New York: John Wiley & Sons, Inc.

Hill, J. W., & Kolb *Research, 8,* 311-332.

Houran, J., & Brugger, P. (2000). The need for independent control sites: A methodological suggestion with special reference to haunting and poltergeist field research. *European Journal of Parapsychology, 15,* 30-45.

Masterton, W. L., & Hurley, C. N. (1997). *Chemistry: Principles and Reactions* (3rd Ed.). Fort Worth, TX: Saunders College Publishing.

Morton, R. C. (1892). Record of a haunted house. *Proceedings of the Society for Psychical, 8,* 311–332.

Osis, K. (1982). New equipment for ASPR research on apparitions. *ASPR Newsletter, 8,* p. 1.

Parsons, S. T., & O'Keeffe, C. (2006). An initial exploration of ambient temperature fluctuations and anomalous experiences. *Proceedings of Presented Papers: The Parapsychological Association 49th Annual Convention* (pp. 335-338). Petaluma, CA: Parapsychological Association, Inc.

Persinger, M. A. (1974). *The Paranormal: Part II Mechanisms and Models.* New York: M.S.S. Information Corporation.

Persinger, M. A. (1985). Geophysical variables and behavior: XXII. The tectonogenic strain continuum of unusual events. *Perceptual and Motor Skills, 60,* 59-65.

Radin, D. I., & Rebman, J. M. (1996). Are phantasms fact or fantasy? A preliminary investigation of apparitions evoked in the laboratory. *Journal of the Society for Psychical Research, 61,* 65-87.

Roll, W. G., & Persinger, M. A. (2001). Investigations of poltergeists and haunts: A review and interpretation. In J. Houran & R. Lange (Eds.) *Hauntings and Poltergeists: Multidisciplinary Perspectives* (pp. 123-163). Jefferson, NC: McFarland & Company.

Roll, W. G., Sheehan, L. C., Persinger, M. A., & Glass, A. Y. (1996). The haunting of White Ranch. *Proceedings of Presented Papers: The Parapsychological Association 39th Annual Convention* (pp. 279-294). Durham, NC: Parapsychological Association, Inc.

Terhune, D. B., Ventola, A., & Houran, J. (2007). An analysis of contextual variables and the incidence of photographic anomalies at an alleged haunt and a control site. *Journal of Scientific Exploration, 21,* 99-120.

Turner, K. H. (1970). A South Yorkshire haunt. *Journal of the Society for Psychical Research, 45,* 325-353.

Tyrrell, G. N. M. (1953/1961). *Science and Psychical Phenomena/Appari-*

tions. New Hyde Park, NY: University Books.

Wiseman, R., Watt, C., Stevens, P., Greening, E., & O'Keeffe, C. (2003). An investigation into alleged 'hauntings.' *British Journal of Psychology, 94,* 195-211.

Bryan Williams *is a Native American student at the University of New Mexico, where his undergraduate studies have focused on physiological psychology and physics. He is a student affiliate of the Parapsychological Association, a student member of the Society for Scientific Exploration, and a co-moderator of the Psi Society, a Yahoo electronic discussion group for the general public that is devoted to parapsychology. He has been an active contributor to the Global Consciousness Project since 2001.*

Annalisa Ventola *is a pianist, keyboard instructor, amateur photographer, and writer/researcher in the field of parapsychology. Her published research is primarily the area paranormal belief and haunting phenomena. She is the executive secretary of the Parapsychological Association and an associate member of the Center for Research on Consciousness and Anomalous Psychology at Lund University, Sweden.*

Mike Wilson *is an amateur scientist, technical writer, and business analyst. He is a council member on the Society of Scientific Exploration and is a moderator for the SSE, Psi Society, and Psi Research Yahoo Groups.*

Satan for a Master:
An Example of a Witch Trial Case in Fribourg (Switzerland) at the End of the Middle Ages[1]
By Patrick J. Gyger
Translation: Jessica Edwards

Despite the persistent cliché that links the Middle Ages with witch hunts, it is relatively common knowledge today that the organized persecution of witchcraft appeared very late in the medieval period and became more prevalent during the modern era. It is less well known that it was in Romandy (French-speaking Switzerland) that the organization of large-scale accusations against men and women under suspicion of heretic practices first began.[2] The region of Fribourg was at the heart of this process. In the late 14th and early 15th centuries, the city authorities twice made official appeals to the Bishop of Lausanne, summoning inquisitors to help them solve cases involving Vaudois heretics (a sect based on the sermons of Pierre Valdo, a preacher from 12th century Lyon).[3] In doing so, the Fribourg authorities contributed considerably to the creation of a permanent inquisition in Romandy. From the second half of the 1430s, the focus of their attention shifted from Vaudois heretics, to witches and sorcerers. From then on, the Fribourg authorities led their own witch-hunt, without calling for the inquisitor.[4] So at the end of the 15th century, the judicial authorities of Fribourg had the latitude to judge heresy as they pleased. This period would thus be important for the consolidation of the social imagination around the Witches' Sabbat and its rituals.

By looking at judicial sources in Fribourg during the last quarter of the 15th century, it is therefore possible to gain a picture of witchcraft that can help us understand more generally the process and fears linked to these practices at a pivotal time and place.

Sources and Context

The sources used for this study come from a collection evocatively titled the "Black Books" (*Livres noirs*).[5] The volumes studied are located in the Archives of the State of Fribourg and contain numerous documents relating to the justice administered by the city's authorities from the end of the 15th century.[6] The Black Books are exceptional, not only for the number of cases recorded and the fact that each confession is followed by the judges' decision, but for their form.[7] An entry in the Black Books is a sign of a criminal investigation by the authorities. The records in this register are thus a part of a particular procedure reserved for individuals responsible for seriously reprehensible acts. There is evidence of a clear will to group into one volume the names and machinations of a specific part of the population, making this collection a *de facto* "register of infamy." Even the name "Black Book" reinforces this negative image, as black was considered the color of sin and death. In this respect, the Black Books may be regarded as the equivalent of today's criminal record and seem to embody the defendants' transgressions and the fate that awaited them.

It should be noted that only crimes appear in these volumes, as opposed to misdemeanors. The term "crime" indicates more serious offenses that warranted corporal punishment (*poena sanguinis*) and, more specifically, the death penalty. Those guilty of infringements punishable only by fines, for example, are not mentioned.

At Fribourg, judicial power was concentrated in the hands of the bourgeoisie. Its most powerful members held the reins of the administration. The authorities showed a strong desire to arbitrate and tended to interfere in any affair—even private—that endangered the smooth workings of the seigniory.

As a result, the direction of criminal procedures depended on a dozen individuals (state prosecutor, burgomaster, and councilors), who studied the grounds that could lead to a case being opened. They willingly relied on denunciations and attributed considerable weight to accusations of complicity coming from criminals. They determined the nature of the sentence incurred (a simple fine, or corporal, even capital, punishment) before even hearing the defendant. The officers of the court recommended whether the use of torture was appropriate, evaluated the prisoner's responsibility, and judged, more often than not without seeking proof other than his or her own testimony, if without too great a risk they could simply make the defendant promise not to offend again, before freeing him or her. If not, they evaluated the case's particularities before choosing the sentence and how it was to be executed. In this type of inquisitory trial there was no question of the presumption of innocence.

The decisions made at each of these stages were generally crucial for the life of the defendant, who had no means of defense other than his or her own testimony. For example, it was impossible to ask witnesses to give testimony suggesting the defendant's innocence, or to appeal the verdict. The deliberations about a case took into account the legislation, the judges' prior experiences, and sometimes the context of the matter and the defendant himself or herself. But in no circumstances did they serve to determine the guilt of the defendant, which had already been established during interrogations and before consigning the case to the Black Book. The ministers of justice had only to agree on the form of punishment to inflict upon the criminal. This decision was made in a small room, part of which was enclosed by a curtain. This would be opened during sentencing to reveal a monumental painting—a Last Judgment motif—intended to impress and to legitimize the judgment. Indeed, "while the judges sit, at the same hour God is sitting in his divine tribunal."[8]

The procedure would generally take less than a week between the defendant's capture and his punishment, in part due to the simplicity of the process, but also due too the desire to limit the cost of justice, which increased with time spent in prison.

So, the system was inherently severe, and the processes involved led to a certain intransigence. However, the councilors could not be said to be seeking harsh verdicts arbitrarily, and bringing a case to trial did not invariably lead to the confession of capital crimes. It should be noted that the investigation, which likely played a decisive role in the charging of a suspect, does not appear in our sources, thus today we possess only some of the elements available to the ministers of justice in their evaluation of criminal affairs.

General Profile of the Criminals

The range of crimes mentioned in the Black Books of Fribourg is very broad, and the most important offenses are well represented. Thus the Black Books enable us to observe criminal habits, isolate characteristics common to outlaws, establish the motivation for criminal acts, as well as to determine whether crime was omnipresent in society, or confined to certain circles. In addition, through the judgments pronounced, we can observe the methods used to curb certain excesses and the response that the court wished to give to those who endangered the stability of the State.

Over a period of thirty years these documents reveal a wide variety of delinquents, comprised predominantly of individuals from disadvantaged backgrounds. The accused were mainly common people touched by poverty, most of whom could be described as ordinary. The most dangerous outlaws are, almost without exception, mercenaries who were accused several times of banditry in the Black Books, particularly during the periods directly following one of the major conflicts in which soldiers from Fribourg participated.[9] They distinguished themselves by their propensity for violence.

Genuine dissidents, vagabonds, and vagrants are rare among the criminals charged, even though they would have undoubtedly raised suspicion at the time. The authorities were often content to throw them in the dungeon for a few days—perhaps as a preventative measure—before setting them free with a clear warning to leave the vicinity of the town.

Thus, aside from dangerous mercenaries and people displaying clear moral abnormalities,[10] the Black Books do not reflect a desire to exclude certain categories of person from society. However, there are exceptions, first and foremost the heretics.

Witches and Heretics

Witchcraft, which is usually referred to as *vauderie*[11] in the Black Books, was considered a crime against governmental authority. According to the criminal registers, Fribourg at the end of the 15th century appears to be relatively quiet in terms of charges of heresy. However, this impression is somewhat invalidated by the town's official accounts, which interestingly contain multiple instances of evidence of witchcraft.[12] For example, in 1479, a vagabond and four women were arrested because "they seem to be *Vaudois*." In 1482 the manager of the Fribourg public bath was paid for shaving a man "who seemed to be *Vaudois*," possibly in order to uncover a diabolical mark. In the same year, several robes were made—presumably to be worn at the stake—for a group of *Vaudois*, whose names and number are unknown. However, we cannot be certain that these defendants were executed. In the last quarter of the 15th century, it is probable that a number of people suspected of heretical practices were interrogated, sometimes using torture, before being released. Nonetheless, though it is not possible to determine the precise extent of witch hunting in the last quarter of the 15th century in Fribourg, the trials recorded in the Black Books are exemplary. The confession of Jehanneta is at the center of one of those affairs:

"Tuesday the twentieth of August of the year one thousand four hundred and ninety-three, in the presence of the wise, provident and prudent councilors of Fribourg Jehan Mussilier, Pierre Ramu, Jehan

Cordeir, Hans Espagniod, Guilliame Gastrod, Wilhelm Reyff and Hans Techterman, *grand sautier* of Fribourg, Jehanetta, widow of Estinien Lasne de Vacheresse, has confessed that, because of the great sorrow she felt because her husband beat her, she went one night to a wood, stood on a rock, and cried out that God or the Devil should help her. Then came to her someone of the name of Sathanaz, of dark appearance, who asked her what she wanted and what was the cause of her distress. She replied that she was very unhappy because her husband would not stop beating her. Sathanaz then told her that if she wanted to believe him, take him as her master and renounce God, he would comfort her and her husband would no longer beat her. At that moment, she renounced God, took Sathanaz as her master and, to give him homage, kissed his backside, before giving him three hairs from her head as a pledge.

"Furthermore, she has confessed that after that she frequented and went to the sect which was held in an old ruined castle, called Berney, and this for two years. Their master Sathanaz summoned them twice a week, on Wednesdays and Fridays, and he gave them short sticks upon which they rode to the sect. If, by chance, they did not want to go he would beat them severely. When it was time to leave they rode these sticks and each went back to his or her dwelling.

Furthermore, she and her accomplices (who are named hereafter) would meet on these days at the sect around midnight and when they were all assembled, they would start first to dance and to give themselves over to festivities, before their master Sathanaz brought them food. And one of the members of the sect, named Pierre Sessel, of Larringes, was their cook.

Furthermore, one of her accomplices, called Jehan Villie, took a young pregnant woman in his arms and squeezed her so strongly that, shortly afterwards, she gave birth to a son, who was not baptized. After his burial, they went secretly to unearth him while still fresh and took him to the sect, where they roasted him and ate him. They ate several other children there, but she did not know where they came from: nonetheless, they had not had a baptism, as they have no power over baptized children. Furthermore, when they were at the sect, they copulated, without however giving themselves over to unnatural practices.

"Furthermore, a number of people who were in the sect have been burned and executed by the court.

"Furthermore, one of the accomplices named Jehan Livret (who has been burned), knew how to make people and animals fall ill using a grease with which he would rub them, then he would hit them with a stick and they were immediately ill. If they were not cared for, they would very probably die. However, when they were presented to her, Jehanneta could easily heal them using incantations that she knows, which have been ineffectual since her detainment by the court.

"Furthermore, the last husband that she had in this town knew full well that she was a heretic. And here are those belonging to that sect: Pierre Morat, Berthet Daman, the wife of Gros Boney de Larringes, the wife of Magniens, Jehan Guilliame du Bois, the son of Niccod de la Vernaz, as well as several others who have been executed by the court and whom she does not remember."[13]

Like this case, the two other examples of heresy found in the Black Books describe key motifs of the Sabbat, and the personalities of the accused. The defendant, usually a woman, confessed having turned to the Devil out of pique or poverty. She renounced God and declared allegiance to the Devil with the kiss of shame (*osculum infame*) and would have paid homage to him with gifts. According to her, the "enemy" could take the form of a seductive man or of a cat. However, he would rapidly reveal his true nature, not only by sometimes taking a more worrying form but by being a deceiver. He would not keep his promises, hit his servants and gave money, which would turn into leaves.

The accusation of witchcraft also included several serious crimes apart from the act of heresy itself, as the sect gave itself over to debauchery and cannibalism (preferably of children, but on one occasion the roasted flesh of a woman). Also, after having engaged upon a ritual with the Devil as host and flying through the air on sticks, the adepts would invoke hail to try and destroy the harvest, and kill young people or animals with powders or other substances.

These statements are typical of witch confessions in Fribourg or in Romandy, during this period, or slightly earlier. They draw on motifs found in the learned tradition, with their procession of evil spells and the fears attached to them. It is therefore likely that the defendants repeated what they had heard in sermons or in public readings of confessions marking the conclusion of previous trials of heretics.[15] Therefore, the accused simply reproduced the beliefs of the inquisitors. The heretics' world mirrors that of the Catholic orthodoxy, in that the Devil works to destroy Christian society and the Church. After having imagined a reality and spread belief in it, the judicial authorities acquire by torture the confirmation of its existence. As Martine Ostorero, specialist in witchcraft in Romandy, has pointed out, "the beliefs which were spread had very real effects. In the witch trials, you could be condemned for a belief held by those judging you, but which you ended up sharing. In a legal sense, the inquisition was innovative: in the accusatory procedure previously applied, the plaintiff had to prove the guilt of the one that he was accusing, or risk incurring the punishment which the latter would have undergone. But to prove the crime of witchcraft was to identify oneself as belonging to the sect. So another procedure had to be found. This was to be investigation and confession."[16]

In the end, confession was all that mattered, the guilt of the defendant having been established solely through his or her own statements. And in the last stages of the trial, when it was time to pronounce the verdict, the reputation of the defendant and the accusations made against him and her were not taken into consideration. Even the investigation became secondary, as its main aim was the complete and reliable confession of the defendant.

A Verdict Without Appeal

The decision-making took place before any intervention from the defendant's friends and family, and even before the councilors substantially evaluated the accused. It would seem that they attempted to set aside any subjective criteria in their verdict. Moreover, the ministers of justice would often pronounce a sentence whilst fully aware that it would not be carried out. By distinguishing sentence and punishment, the councilors seem to have been protecting themselves against possible objections, by basing the judgment on well-established customs. Above all, the judges affirmed their power over life and death by having the sentence read at the execution site itself. They could then clearly show their mercy or, on the contrary, their imperviousness, by commuting or administering the specific punishment they had chosen.

Punishments used in Fribourg at the end of the 15th century—whether they affected the honor, the body, or the soul of the criminal—appear to reflect two types of attitude held by the authorities towards outlaws. When the authorities believed it possible to rehabilitate a petty delinquent, they would show clemency. The involvement of the culprit's family and friends would thus be of prime importance in their decision, as it showed that the condemned person still had a place in the community, as opposed to someone whom nobody was concerned about. If the accused was young, there would be hope that he or she might still change their behavior and abandon the path of wickedness upon which they had embarked. This is why on August 22, 1493, the councilors of Fribourg had Glaudo Fudran cross the town with the executioner flogging him, and then set him free.[17] Under the law he deserved a harsher punishment—hanging—as he was found guilty of two thefts. More importantly, he had begun to frequent criminal circles. Despite all this, the court gave him a second chance, as his parents and friends had accepted responsibility for him.

However, that same day, the criminal court made up of the same councilors mercilessly sent Jehanneta, the above-mentioned witch, to the stake. Her case had been heard just two days earlier at a single questioning. Although a certain type of clemency was sometimes shown to women, who were usually spared the most severe punishments such as the wheel or the scaffold, the specific nature of this crime took precedence over the defendant, and in this case the stake could not be avoided. In the eyes of the court, there was a category of criminal who had passed a limit of forgiveness, and the most severely penalized offenses were those committed by heretics. Moreover, heretics were not entitled to a grave. As the culprit's body did not lie in consecrated ground, the salvation of his or her soul came into question. The body was destroyed by the fire, and any remains not burnt to a cinder were buried under a layer of quicklime, though often all that was left were ashes to be thrown to the wind.

Despite these relatively exceptional cases, it must be noted that as a general rule, criminality remained anchored in the banality of everyday life. It was—particularly in the rural world—linked with money problems, sexual appetites, and passing rages. Consequently, judges' decisions usually simply underlined the gap between those who were already partly excluded from the mainstream and the rest of the population. Thus, not only do the Black Books give a very clear picture of the social imaginary of the Sabbat in this period, but they also provide an early insight into the groups who would increasingly become suspected of witchcraft. At the end of the 15th century, a woman showing signs of ostracism (old age, solitude linked to widowhood, etc.) tended to be viewed as the Devil's preferred agent.

In the end, there is nothing very surprising in this. Difference and marginality drew the attention and concern of a criminal court dominated by a group of *Bourgeois*. This group protected the interests and the advantages of their peers, in so doing echoed an oligarchic regime that they contributed to putting in place. Moreover, the strict application of the inquisitory procedure was the keystone of this policy. By facilitating the arrest and the condemnation of those whom the judges considered to be potential enemies of authority, that authority was strengthened. However, by trying to protect themselves and concentrate judicial power in a limited number of hands, they fostered a system that helped pave the way for decades of witch hunts not only in Romandy Switzerland, but in the whole of Europe.

Notes

1. Numerous elements of this article are taken from Patrick J. Gyger, *L'épée et la corde: Criminalité et justice à Fribourg (1475-1505)*, Lausanne 1998 (Cahiers Lausannois d'Histoire Médiévale 22), which the reader may consult for further details. For a global view of witchcraft in the modern era (1450-1750) see *Encyclopaedia of Witchcraft: The Western Tradition*, 4 vol., ABC-Clio, 2006, edited by Richard M. Golden.

2. The repression of witchcraft in Romandy/French-speaking Switzerland has been the subject of important studies for several years, conducted principally from the University of Lausanne (the very recent international conference "Witch hunts and demonology: from discourse to practice (Middle Ages—Modern Era)" can testify to this). See the works published within the framework of this research: *Inquisition et sorcellerie en Suisse romande. Le registre Ac 29 des Archives cantonales vaudoises (1438 - 1528)*, texts collected by Martine Ostorero and Kathrin Utz Tremp in collaboration with Georg Modestin, CLHM, vol. 41, Lausanne, 2007, 561 pages, *L'imaginaire du sabbat. Édition critique des textes les plus anciens (1430 c.-1440 c.)*, collected by Martine Ostorero, Agostino Paravicini Bagliani, Kathrin Utz Tremp, in collaboration with Catherine Chène, CLHM, vol. 26, Lausanne, 1999, Georg Modestin, *Le diable chez l'évêque. Chasse aux sorciers dans le diocèse de Lausanne (vers 1460)*, CLHM, vol. 25, Lausanne, 1999, Laurence Pfister, *L'enfer sur terre. Sorcellerie à Dommartin (1498)*, CLHM, vol. 20, Lausanne, 1997, Sandrine Strobino, *Françoise sauvée des flammes? Une Valaisanne accusée de sorcellerie au XVe siècle*, CLHM, vol. 18, Lausanne, 1996, Eva Maier, *Trente ans avec le diable. Une nouvelle chasse aux sorciers sur la Riviera lémanique (1477-1484)*, CLHM, vol. 17, Lausanne, 1996, Martine Ostorero, *"Folâtrer avec les démons". Sabbat et chasse aux sorciers à Vevey (1448)*, CLHM, vol. 15, Lausanne, 1995, Fabienne Taric Zumsteg, *Les sorciers à l'assaut du village. Gollion (1615-1631)*, Etudes d'histoire moderne 2, Editions du Zèbre, Lausanne, 2000, Pierre- Han Choffat, *La sorcellerie comme exutoire. Tensions et conflits locaux*, CLHM 1, Lausanne, 1989.

3. The creation of a permanent inquisition in Romandy goes right back to 1267, when Pope Clement IV asked the Dominicans to set up an inquisition in the dioceses of Besançon, Geneva, Lausanne, Sion, Toul, Metz and Verdun. But it was only at the end of the 14th century that it truly became operational, with the first trial against the Vaudois heretics, which took place in Fribourg (Diocese of Lausanne) in 1399. For this, the Fribourg authorities consulted the Bishop of Lausanne, who in turn mandated the Dominican Humbert Franconis, member of the Dominican monastery of Lausanne and

inquisitor. In 1430, the *Fribourgeois* made a further appeal to an inquisitor: Ulric de Torrenté, also from the Dominican monastery of Lausanne. Once again they used the official channel by sending their chancellor to the Bishop of Lausanne in order to ask for the inquisitor and the Episcopal representative.

4. This independence was strengthened when Fribourg gained freedom from Savoyard control to become a sovereign state in 1477, before joining the Swiss confederation in 1481.

5. These volumes are written in French, German, and Latin. For a detailed description of these sources, cf. Gyger, pp. 13-19 and pp. 231-253; for the edition of the French and Latin sections, Ibid. pp. 255-357.

6. The name "Black Books" (*Schwarzbücher*) is used to indicate the first *Thurnrodels*, a very significant corpus of thirty-eight volumes of unequalled length, ranging from 1475 to 1799. In the State of Fribourg Archives (AEF), they are itemized in the R1 inventory, pp. 78-79, n° 1-38. The initial three Black Books cover the period from 1475-1505 and form the first complete series of *Thurnrodels*, while the fourth treats the years 1516-1521.

7. The Black Books mainly record investigations comprising the protocol of one or more interrogations of a suspect (*process*), followed by a note indicating the execution of the sentence. Most of these documents are short, from a few lines to several pages depending on the seriousness of the case, the number of crimes described and the details given.

8. German customary from the 14th century cited by Robert Jacob, *Images de la justice: essai sur l'iconographie judiciaire du Moyen Age à l'âge classique*, Paris 1994, p. 61.

9. The Burgundy, Souabe and Milan wars (1475-1476 and 1499-1503). The mercenaries appearing in the Black Books are therefore distinguished by their frequent voyages in the Vaud region, in Savoy or in Northern Italy. These individuals clearly form the most brutal category of criminals.

10. Mainly those whose sexuality was judged to be against nature (guilty of bestiality, homosexuality, or polygamy).

11. Indeed, *Vaudois* heresy and witchcraft are associated and confused. See, concerning the use of terms for witches, Ostorero *Folâtrer*, p. 174.

12. Accounts of the Treasurers of the State of Fribourg, n°111, 130, 132, 137, 154, 157, 160 and 197.

13. See Gyger, p. 310.

14. Practices very similar to those referred to here would be confessed to a few years later by other witches of Fribourg: in 1520 and 1521, the confessions of Gredi De Riaulx and Glauda Perottet, collected in the fourth *Thurnrodel*, contain similar elements to those found in the first three Black Books: the sacrifice of one hen a year in homage, a kiss on the tail of the Devil in the shape of a cat, transformation of money, use of greases and powders, the making of hail using a fountain, etc. (*Thurnrodel* 4, pp. 39-42, Ibid., pp. 52-54).

15. Jehanneta had probably attended such readings of death sentences, which is

why she would have mentioned executions.

16. *Allez Savoir*, juin 2006, Université de Lausanne, pp. 21-22.
17. See Gyger, p. 312.

Patrick J. Gyger *is a trained historian and is currently the Director of Maison d'Ailleurs (www.ailleurs.ch), Museum of Science Fiction, Utopia and Extraordinary Voyages in Yverdon-les-Bains, Switzerland. From 2001-2005 he was artistic director of Utopiales, the International Science-Fiction festival in Nantes, and has worked on several volumes that link reality and the imaginary, such as* De beaux lendemains? Histoire, société et politique dans la science-fiction, Great Days to Come? History, Society and Politics in Science-Fiction *(with Gianni Haver; Lausanne, Antipodes, 2002) and* Les voitures volantes: Souvenirs d'un futur rêvé *(Ed. Favre, 2005).*

Prometheus' Curse:
Carlos Castaneda, Whitley Strieber, and the Perils of the Literary Shaman
By Aeolus Kephas

Over the years, Carlos Castaneda (who died in 1999) wrote a series of books during the 1960s and '70s chronicling his apprenticeship with "Yaqui sorcerer" don Juan Matus in Mexico. These sold in their millions and stirred up a mountain of speculation and controversy, (1) while having incalculable influence on "alternative" Western thought. Whitley Strieber (alleged alien abductee and author of *Communion, Transformation,* and *The Key*) has also enjoyed best seller status, and his most recent works, *The Grays* and *2012*, novels inspired by the author's supposed real-life encounters with alien beings, are currently being developed as major Hollywood motion picture productions. Though seeming to occupy quite different areas of the anomaly spectrum, there are interesting parallels between these two authors that merit further exploration.

Both Castaneda and Strieber were apparently singled out by mysterious parties to undergo an extraordinary initiation process and bring account of it to the world. Without the intervention of don Juan Matus and his party of sorcerers, it's doubtful we would ever have heard of Castaneda. Likewise Strieber: although he was already a best-selling author (of horror fiction) before his alien encounter of 1985, it was only with the publication of *Communion*, in 1986, that Strieber established himself as one of the most puzzling and original writers of our time. In the field he has chosen – or been chosen—to write, that of UFOs and alien visitation, Strieber is probably the current leading exponent.

Like Castaneda, Strieber has a gift for bringing almost inconceivable concepts and experiences into the realm of everyday reality. His work forms a bridge between two apparently (or previously) inseparable realities and invites the reader to cross over into the Land of Oz. And although Strieber's body of work cannot compete with Castaneda's as a storehouse of esoteric wisdom, it serves a similar function: that of describing—and thereby helping to consolidate – a perception of reality (and of humanity's predicament) utterly at odds with the current consensus view.

The other obvious parallel to be drawn between Castaneda and Strieber is that both authors have been denounced as hoaxers, opportunists, and just plain liars. Without going into detail, there are a considerable number of inconsistencies, if not glaring contradictions, to be found in the work of both writers, and these have led skeptics to deduce that the accounts were "cut from whole cloth." I may as well say, right off the bat, that I consider such an idea untenable. In the case of both Castaneda and Strieber, there is simply too much in their work of obvious merit—too much insight, depth, and sheer novelty—for me to believe, even for a moment, that these accounts are wholly invented.

Even if one accepts the notion that the inconsistencies were deliberately placed as a kind of double-bluff (i.e., if the accounts were fiction, why include such glaring contradictions?), viewing these works as "simple" fiction (the best of Strieber, and all of Castaneda) raises far more questions than it answers. I believe the answer is far less straightforward or convenient than any simple verdict of "fact" or "fiction." Since both authors are recounting their initiation into imaginal realms, in which the laws of physics are closer to quantum mechanics than those of Newton (i.e., more microcosmic than macro-, more subjective dream reality than objective consensus reality), the shaky, amorphous quality of both Strieber's and Castaneda's accounts actually confirms their authenticity rather than undermines it.

Few writers have made such a fearless and thorough public exploration of their psyches as Strieber has. "Objectively" speaking, *Communion*—and its follow-up *Transformation*—remain to date the most compelling and insightful personal testimonies of "alien abduction" currently on record. The apparently naked honesty with which Strieber reports his experiences, and the raw emotion with which he imbues them, make for powerfully disturbing reading. Strieber's willingness to refrain from judgment, to resist the almost overpowering urge to "explain" his experiences and make them fit into ordinary understanding (i.e., by assuming he is dealing with aliens from outer space), make it clear he is not merely peddling a doctrine, or if he is, is extremely cunning in his salesmanship. Strieber testifies to the ways in which he has been transformed by his experiences, despite his emotional resistance, and the eventual benefits he was able to reap from them. If taken at face value, Strieber's accounts are testimony to the way in which these incredibly strange events—by refusing to submit to rational interpretation—forced his consciousness to adapt and evolve in order to survive. Like Castaneda's books, Strieber's works describe one man's slow and traumatic initiation into a separate reality.

As Strieber points out, his experiences (and hence the body of his work to date) are essentially shamanic in nature. They resemble visits to the lower world of the collective unconscious which, however abstract and fantastic, are every bit as real as "objective" reality. Like Castaneda, his desire to share his experience appears to stem from a belief that, far from aberrations, these realities are pertinent to us all. The alien interface which Strieber describes and the separate reality of Castaneda are—both authors insist—universal experiences; as such, they are not only available to us but *inescapable*. Strieber's cry in the wilderness is not so much "Repent!" as "Know thyself!" and it is fueled by a certainty that, whatever alien abduction *is*, it is not the exception to human experience but the rule. As Strieber sees it, it is the *active element* in an evolutionary process which, by definition, is not only happening at an individual level but to the species as a whole.

Strieber's missionary zeal has not always enhanced his literary talents, however. After *Transformation* and *Majestic* (an effective novel about the Roswell UFO "crash" and cover-up), he wrote two negligible works in which he seemed to be milking his "alien" experiences for all they were worth. Perhaps he needed the money, because *Breakthrough* and *The Secret School* (and also *The Communion Letters*, a collection of correspondences from his readers, edited by Strieber and his wife, Anne) are almost entirely lacking the intensity and depth of his first two books. But then, since his abduction experiences allegedly tailed off soon after *Transformation* (according to Strieber, they have yet to recur), there was very little left for him to report. This didn't stop him writing books, however, and Strieber has occasionally been accused of betraying an opportunistic streak. Weird things seem to happen to him at regular intervals, and even when they don't, he finds new theories by which to re-examine his experiences and generate renewed interest in them. This may be a genuine desire to understand them, just as it may be simple mercenary tactics. Or it may stem from a neurotic need for attention. Perhaps Strieber summons up imaginal crises and revelations whenever he needs to spice up his life and give him something new to write about?

As it happens, a similar charge has been leveled at Castaneda, namely, that once his "tales of power" had apparently reached a natural end (when don Juan left the world), he began to access buried memories of "the left side," and was able to spin off a bunch more books. This is a fairly unimaginative theory, however, since (unlike with some of Strieber's work) there is nothing in the books themselves that suggests such desperate subterfuge. *The Art of Dreaming* notwithstanding, Castaneda's works continued to astonish, and even surpass themselves, with each subsequent book.

For the purposes of this study, and for the sake of argument, I am going to assume that, however unreliable their accounts might be, and despite any evidence of "tampering," both authors *were* genuinely reporting experiences that *happened*, and not merely inventing them or suffering from hallucinations. Any thorough examination of the evidence (if it includes the knowledge contained in the writings themselves, which debunkers rarely do) reveals this to be by far the most likely conclusion. Put simply: there is far too much *truth* in these books for them not to have at least *some* basis in fact.

If we allow for this, we can state the following: both Castaneda's and Strieber's gift is for relaying experiences and knowledge *passed on from elsewhere*. Their greatest insights, although they assuredly come through them, do not appear to come *from* them. This can be said of all great artists, in one way or another, but the problem with Strieber and Castaneda is that their source is not God but (apparently) *godlike beings* whom they have had *direct* contact with. In a way, if both authors are to be even partially believed, they are little more than glorified postmen for superior intelligence. (2) For a best-selling author to be reduced to the role of cosmic postman can be tough for a proud intellect to come to grips with, most especially if the message he delivers goes largely unheeded (as seems the case particularly with Strieber).

"What writing produces when it is pressed to its extremes is a sense of isolation, an alienation, a cosmic aloneness in which nature and religion are lost." —William Irwin Thompson, *Coming Into Being*

Interestingly, both authors' way of dealing with the soul-shattering truths they were forced to confront—both within and outside them—was to write them down. Castaneda became a figure of fun among the sorcerers for his relentless note-taking, and Strieber has managed to turn just about every major experience of his life (including family tragedies) into source material for his books and website journal. The intellect is the best defense against the onslaught of magickal reality, and writing about their experiences may have been these men's way of distancing themselves from them. The danger of this is obvious. Writing fosters the illusion of having assimilated and understood an experience when the opposite is really the case: writing is a means *not* to assimilate experience fully, to keep it at bay. Intellectual understanding is theoretical and not practical—it's all in the head.

It seems likely that Castaneda was allowed access to the sorcerers' world not because he necessarily belonged there, but because he had the right kind of "journalistic" (i.e., intellectual) bent to pass on his experiences to the rest of humanity. The same may be true of Strieber. It may be that he has been exposed to a level of intensity, power, and revelation that would unhinge the sturdiest of minds, expressly in order to relay information to the world, and that his own assimilation of these experiences is inessential to his passing them on. In which case, neither Castaneda's nor Strieber's testimonies are what they appear to be; or rather, they are *exactly* what they appear to be (one man's rational struggle with impossible experiences), but also something else entirely: a subtle and unwitting description of the pitfalls the intellect creates for itself, once having strayed into the realm of the imaginal.

If there is one recurring flaw in Strieber's work (which separates it from Castaneda's), it relates to an earnestness and gravity that tends to preclude much humor or playfulness. Castaneda may have taken himself too seriously, but if so it was more than compensated for by the playful jibes of the sorcerers he describes. This is true to some extent of Strieber's "aliens" (who are mischievous in the extreme); but since there is obviously less of an overlap between Strieber and the "visitors" and Castaneda and his sorcerers (who are at least of the same species!), much of the humor of Strieber's accounts seems to bubble up almost *despite* him. Unlike don Juan Matus, Strieber doesn't seem too fond of jokes. He appears to have been too severely traumatized by his experiences to ever make light of them, and at some deep level, Strieber is clearly divided against himself. This divided allegiance acts like a dead weight that inadvertently distorts his message. There is something heavy about much of Strieber's writings, and it is most evident—and most troubling—in this almost complete lack of humor.

A lack of humor is often a dead giveaway for an excess of self-importance, and if anything is guaranteed to distort and corrupt "sacred wisdom," it is self-importance. When it comes to conveying apocalyptic truths to an unreceptive public, the danger is not so much that someone will decide to "kill the messenger"—though this can happen too—but that the messenger becomes so puffed up at being "chosen" that he confuses the gravity of the transmission with his own self-importance, and distorts the message in the process of delivering it. This is a surefire way to alienate both the people the message is intended for and whoever or whatever provided it to begin with. In the end, the burden and responsibility of the message may well prove fatal to the person chosen to deliver it.

Castaneda wrote to the bitter end, yet if we are to give any credence to accounts of his final years (primarily Amy Wallace's *Sorcerer's Apprentice*, which oddly enough Strieber reviewed), the truth he had worked so hard to bring to the world slipped through his own fingers. Apparently, exposure to the incomprehensible forces of sorcery proved too much for him: unwilling or unable to relinquish his self-importance, he was defeated by the third enemy of a man of knowledge, succumbed to the temptations of power, and became (in the words of don Juan) a "cruel, capricious man." Strieber does not *appear* to be treading the same path; missionary zeal aside, he is not playing the role of guru yet. He is warming to the role of "prophet of doom," however, and since the kind of experiences he has undergone, or believes he has undergone, are bound to traumatize anyone, it is difficult to say how close to the edge he is.

It may be that the same formidable intellect that allowed Castaneda (and Strieber) to communicate these energetic truths made them unable, finally, to fully assimilate them. In the first of Castaneda's books, *The Teachings of Don Juan*, a third of the work is devoted to an unreadable appendix called "A Structural Analysis," in which the author attempts to wrestle the imaginal realities (which he has just recounted so splendidly) down to the rubber mat of reason. Exactly so far as he succeeds in this endeavor, does he strip the experiences of all their magic, power, and meaning. In the process, he revealed himself as an unwitting clown, a rational lunatic, dancing while Infinity took pot-shots at his feet.

According to don Juan Matus, a man of knowledge is someone who has erased every last trace of personal history, and with it the personal self. If there is no more nor less to the path of knowledge than this, then with his intensely romantic works, Castaneda may have unwittingly glorified and mystified an incredibly simple (though monumentally difficult) accomplishment. Such mystification and glorification would be inextricably bound up with the fact that Castaneda could not attain this primary goal himself. His works might then be seen as his attempt to erase his personal history by writing it down, and by reinventing it. Since, judging by the evidence of his life, he failed in this task, his books remain contaminated by that history, like pure water that has passed through a dirty filter. Brilliant and inspired as they are, the books are not to be trusted; or rather, they should not be taken entirely at face value. (3)

Both Castaneda and Strieber were permitted an extremely rare audience with a very specific kind of "royalty": Castaneda with superhuman sorcerers, Strieber with "aliens." But it's possible they were only granted this audience because *someone* was required to pass specific information (information of gravest urgency) onto humankind. If such were the case, then perhaps neither author was actually "worthy" of (i.e., ready for) the secret knowledge they were given. Perhaps they were even chosen partially for this very limitation, chosen because, as intellectually sophisticated Western males, they were equipped to present the knowledge in a way that would be easily digestible to the general public. Although the message was not intended for just anyone (only a select few would be able to fully understand it), it would have to be made accessible to all. This way, the message could be enjoyed, dismissed, or ignored as a clever yarn, disingenuous hoax, or senseless gibberish, respectively, by those who failed to decipher its true meaning.

Neither Castaneda nor Strieber presented their works as fiction—on the contrary—yet they were cunning enough to make sure they *read* as fiction. As such, their books are in a sense indistinguishable from fiction. I'd wager that this is a major reason for all the confusion and skepticism, because anything that looks this much like a yarn must *be* a yarn. But perhaps this was also part of the subterfuge. For it allows more literal-minded readers, those unable to entertain the subtle, subjective nature of imaginal truth, to dismiss the books, based on purely *circumstantial* evidence (the many contradictions). This subterfuge might have been considered necessary, not only for the protection of the message, but that of the messenger also (and the public); for if he were recognized as what he was—a spy for the imaginal among common folk—he would be dispatched at once. (4)

The temptation to succumb to a sense of power and uniqueness is great. Prophets are usually considered insane and often wind up that way. The combination of exposure to divine knowledge with frustration, anger, and despair in the face of the world's incomprehension and indifference often leads to self-righteous superiority. Likewise, the traumatic effects of revelation combined with a complete lack of support from his fellow men is likely to drive the messenger to take refuge in psychotic delusions of grandeur. The only way for the messenger to withstand the pressure and not wind up half-mad with a mixture of paranoia and megalomania (two symptoms exhibited by Castaneda in his final years) is to constantly remind himself that he is *only a messenger*, a carrier of information, with neither power nor responsibility to create (or even interpret) the message. His only task is to deliver it faithfully and withdraw.

Caught between a strange and deeply threatening new reality and an old reality that no longer offers comfort or assurance, that seems increasingly hollow and illusory, is it any wonder if both Strieber and Castaneda took refuge in writing, and in the grand gestures of prophet-gurus? It would have been the only bridge they had between the two worlds, the only way for them to make sense of either. The pitfall is that the tool they are using to protect themselves from madness—the intellect—is the very thing likely to undo them in the end. Writing becomes not so much a bridge between worlds but a refuge *from* them, creating an illusion of power and control so intoxicating it is almost bound to turn into obsession, the neurotic drive for power.

The very gift for which they were chosen as conveyers of forbidden knowledge would make Castaneda and Strieber outcasts, both in the world of men, and the realm of sorcerers and "aliens." Like Mercury, the price of being granted free passage between the realms meant that they belonged to neither. Intellect, like the messenger, like language itself, is a means and not an end; it has no place in the primal realms or the supernal spheres: the one is beneath it, the other beyond it. This is the comedy and tragedy of the word, and why a day comes in the life of every writer when he or she is forced to choose between the illusory control of the written word—being the messenger—and the power and freedom of direct experience: *becoming the message*. He who lives by the pen, dies by the pen.

Notes

1. Castaneda was even called "the godfather of the New Age," an ironic designation, since, unlike Strieber, his works are anything but populist.
2. This is not to say that Strieber lacks imagination—on the contrary, like Castaneda, his accounts are rich in imagery and feeling—but apparently only when inspired by actual individuals and events. Strieber's straight fiction, for example (what I have read of it, and not counting *Majestic* and *2012*), has been unremarkable. His most powerful work by far, a self-published work called *The Key*, is actually (Strieber claims) a transcript of a conversation he had with a godlike being who burst into his hotel room one night in Toronto and proceeded to reveal to him the secrets of the Universe. The book certainly supports Strieber's outlandish claim: whatever its source, Strieber did a commendable job arranging and presenting the information it contains. Yet—if he is to be believed—that's *all* he did: transcribe and pass on the message.

3. The same must be said of Strieber's work, although in Strieber's case there is an added complication (one which I can only touch upon here), relating to his reputed history of child abuse, and his possible affiliations with government organizations. Castaneda may have been to some extent an unwitting patsy of sorcerers, and he may have lost his marbles in the end. But (tensegrity and those last few dodgy years aside), I believe he was serving an authentically magikal tradition. With Strieber, it may be that (wittingly or not) he is serving two masters at once.

4. Nonetheless, the real danger the messenger faces is his own incapacity to shoulder the burden of knowledge. Since he is privy to the inner workings of the imaginal realm, he is obliged to carry experiences which he can share with no one, not even his readership. Since he will be unable to comprehend much of the knowledge he has been granted, so far beyond his experience does it lie, he won't be able to write about it either, so it is solely for him. This is why it is essential that, whatever else, the messenger must not allow his experiences—neither the honor nor the nigh-unbearable pressure of being chosen as divine emissary—to go to his head. To do so will prove fatal in one way or another.

Aeolus Kephas is the author of The Lucid View: Investigations in Occultism, UFOlogy, and Paranoid Awareness *and* Homo Serpiens: An Occult History of DNA from Eden to Armageddon. *Aeolus also writes a blog called "Aeolus Inc." and produces a podcast entitled "Warty Theorems: Identity Deconstruction and Pattern Recognition in the End Times" (as well as another podcast, "Vagabond Blues," under the name Jason Kephas). His work deals with areas of research that test, or even violate, the limits of consensus reality.*

An Exercise in
Transdimensional Zoology:
Speculating on the
Origin of the Chakras
by John F. Caddy

Introduction

A vast literature exists attesting to the "subjective reality" of what has been called qi, prana, orgone, mana, etc.—a diverse array of terms used by a large and growing number of what may be called "energy schools" to describe the same phenomenon. They all appear to have the common objective of manipulating a mysterious essence that I will refer to as qi. Unfortunately, since each school tends to have their own explanations of "spiritual reality," and often their own secret or esoteric traditions, the standardization or sharing of vocabulary or procedures between competing schools is given low priority. All of these schools of practice seem to have their distant origin in shamanism, and the phenomena described by these traditions are beginning to be taken more seriously nowadays, although science still shrinks from addressing them, except as examples of psychiatric self-delusion. Ironically, the tribal societies for which shamanism forms a basis for their knowledge of the natural world are on the point of disappearing.

The integration of the knowledge systems and practice of shamanic and other "energy cults" with science does not appear to be possible following the usual scientific methods. One example will suffice to illustrate the problem: the ubiquity of Occam's Razor as a criterion for judging whether an explanatory hypothesis can be added to the body of scientific knowledge is that it should be the simplest explanation for the phenomenon. The usual implication is that the components of the explanation are material phenomena already accepted by science. This is not the case for qi. In science, new information is added by accretion, piece by piece, as a result of the work of the many specialized disciplines that nowadays make up the body of practitioners. I believe that the extensive body of paranormal phenomena is too large to be tackled in this way. An alternative approach is to accept paranormal experiences at their face value and seek analogies with phenomena in the physical world. The way forward may then be to operate in a similar fashion to the search for a Theory of Everything (TOE), which requires physicists to create logical structures (such as string theory), which for the moment have no chance of physical verification but serve as a conceptual "clothes horse" for future argumentation.

My suggestion therefore is the one I had to adopt as a scientist learning the procedures of several esoteric energy disciplines; in my case, pranic healing in the school of Master Choa Kok Sui, energy induction by Howard Lee, and Shamanic voyaging in the tradition promoted by Michael Harner (1982). I've described these experiences in some detail elsewhere (Caddy 2006) and there is no need to repeat this. Just to say that the mental framework required to achieve results requires us to avoid skepticism, which in my experience projects a low energy field negating the phenomena you wish to experience. (See also the comment of Professor Stewart in the Winter 2005 review:"We know the negative and hostile attitude of other scientists monitoring the experiment is conducive to failure.") One needs to take the axiomatic statements of an energy discipline at their face value, however illogical, and suspend judgement (knowing that judgements alter our perceptions), and assume a priori that the phenomenon is not an illusion. In a parallel logical process, we should attempt to establish what TOE would be needed to support such a non-ordinary phenomenon. Analogies should be looked for between the esoteric phenomena and those documented in the physical world. A general guide in my view was provided by the Ancient Egyptian sage, Hermes Trismegistus, who in reference to the idea of a parallel "spiritual" world, is reported to have said (Freke and Gandy 1989): "As above, so below.... As in the outer, so in the inner....", a conviction repeated in a key text of the Jewish Kabbalah, Zohar: "He made this world to match the world above, and whatever exists above has its counterpart below" (Oxford Dictionary of Quotations). I take this as a useful guide to speculation, meaning that the phenomena established by Science on this physical plane will have their analogies on other planes of reality where a flow of time also exists, and hence the equivalent of thermodynamics, the law of mass action, and evolutionary processes will all apply. My hypothesis is that qi is either the medium for trans-plane communication, or even the basic structural particle on another plane, just as the sub-atomic components of matter operate here. It seems reasonable to suppose that qi forms the structural element underlying paranormal phenomena such as ectoplasm, auras, chakras, meridians, and energy bodies. If time flows elsewhere as in the physical realm, I suppose that a similar diversity of "energetic" entities will have evolved there; many of which will not be intelligent, in the same way that a diversity of organisms has also been produced by evolutionary processes in this realm.

The usual approach taken by those with a scientific background who try to integrate the material world of phenomena with those called "paranormal," is to suggest links with apparent anomalies that exist at the quantum level, such as an observer affecting the outcome of an experiment, and the "entanglement" of particles implying action at a distance. This approach is fine, and these phenomena would be accepted as obvious by any practicing shaman. The fact that string theory requires multiple dimensions may imply superimposition of non-ordinary realms on the four-dimensional world of matter, but it is also consistent with shamanic voyaging to the lower, middle, and upper worlds. While quantum theory has been postulated as a link between science and paranormal phenomena, an alternative approach would be to treat different paranormal phenomena in a manner consistent between themselves, and to develop analogies with phenomena on the physical plane, using the hypothesis offered above by Hermes as an alternative to that provided by a later pre-scientific sage of more enduring repute, William of Occam (1285-1349).

In the following I discuss chakras, energy bodies, and auras; phenomena I have had personal experience of and hence cannot exclude from reality. As noted, these are arguably composed of an immaterial essence similar if not identical to qi. Chakras have been described from earliest times on the Indian subcontinent by Indian yogic schools as vortices of energy that are associated with different points and organs in the human body and appear to be linked in the body to nerve complexes. (See Motoyama 1995 for a review.) The emphasis has been placed on meridians in the Chinese Taoist tradition (e.g. Jwing Ming 1989), but this also refers to "Energy Gates" such as the lower Dan Tien, which seems equivalent to the Manipura chakra, and the upper Dan Tien or 'third eye," which is in the same location as the Ajna chakra of Yogic traditions. Despite differences in emphasis, both Indian and Chinese energy schools see that correcting bodily anomalies requires first the cleansing or removal of blockages at an energetic level before physical healing can occur. Those who have consistently worked with chakras (e.g. Motoyama 1995) consider that they are portals for the flow of energy and information that place a meditator or trancer in contact with parallel planes of reality. These alternative planes are traditionally viewed as multiple in number and may each be accessed through one of the seven main bodily chakras, although a larger number of smaller chakras are also mentioned by some adepts. If we accept that qi is the "currency" for paranormal phenomena, it seems (e.g., Schnieider and Kay 1994), that chakras are analogous to the dissipation structures described by Ilya Prigogine as a feature of the thermodynamics of systems out of equilibrium. Implicit here is the idea that a surplus of energy on one plane may be dispersed across a "membrane" separating it from another. I speculate that this membrane may not be a simple discontinuity but could be a fractal structure with inherent complexity rather than a simple plane surface. This makes it reasonable to regard chakras as phenomena existing within the membrane separating two planes of reality.

I then introduce the yogic phenomenon of the Silver Cord: that "worm hole," which, in moments of ecstasy and inspiration, links the enclave in our physical body that we the spiritual "lodger" inhabit, to that other universe that many religions say we come from.

Although not essential to this argument, I have assumed that the transition between dimensions may be fractal, and hence that this "membrane" may form a habitat, perhaps resembling the boundary of the "Julia Set" described by Mandelbrot (1983) and illustrated by Peitgen and Richter (1986). This would allow dimensional change to occur gradually between planes. Celtic myths describe non-ordinary meetings between inhabitants of different planes as occurring in a "druidical mist." This evokes in me the idea of the "fractal dust" described by the last-mentioned authors. I would suppose that "pores" occur in this membrane, perhaps similar to the "worm holes" of physicists engaged in TOE's and cosmological speculations. The suggestion in my last-cited book was that such pores and the spiraling dissipation structures that the interplane flow of qi would give rise to, may have provided the focus for the orderly accumulation of material at the microscopic level in the first single celled organism, and perhaps is implicit in the origin of life? Is it a coincidence that DNA is also a spiralling molecule, described as a "demon dancer" in micro-video recordings by Pearson (2003) as it rotates actively in the nucleus of the cell? As a zoologist who accepts the reality of qi from personal experience, this tempts me to speculate on our linkage to associated plane(s) where qi energy is dominant. My analogy here is to symbiotic or parasitic phenomena on the physical plane, and to postulate a possible cellular linkage with another plane of reality acting through actively spiraling DNA molecules.

Stages in Chakra evolution?

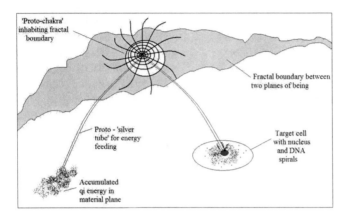

The stages in chakral evolution I hypothesize have similarities to processes on the physical plane, such as the use of tubular structures for predation, mating, egg-laying, and parasitism (examples of which are common and will not be detailed here). I speculate that analogous structures such as the silver tube mentioned in Yogic writings, which link the chakras to other planes of reality may be the end process of an evolutionary sequence that can be mapped out as follows:

• Turbillons of energy (proto-chakras) exist in the fractal membrane separating planes of existence, and are driven by inflows of qi from other planes of existence to our material plane through pores in this membrane; or vice versa. Since these turbillons are made up of qi, they are by definition 'alive'.

• Around the pores where qi enters our plane, accretions of organic matter accumulated and acquired a spiral configuration around the 'micropores' or wormholes to which the microchakras are attached.

• Mimicking the spiraling nature of matter flowing through dissipation structures, organic material and proto-DNA spirals became established around these 'micropores' at the points where qi energy enters the cell. After many aeons, "the Big Birth" occurred, whereby the sack of chemicals containing the micropore split, together with the proto-DNA and the micro-chakra attached to it.

At a later stage, and in parallel with evolution on the material plane, free living chakras acquired a complex wheel-like structure and began to move within the fractal boundary between planes. They are dependent for their existence on locating accumulations of energy on either side of the membrane which they transmit between planes.

- During transmission they function as "turbines" and so accumulate energy/qi in the process.

- Eventually, larger versions of free-living chakras roam the boundary between planes of existence searching for accretions of qi, and become associated with living cells and their aural field. Free-living protochakras "predate" the qi reserves of physical organisms.

- To do so, the predators develop a "silver tube" that enters the energy body of prey organisms on our plane while feeding.

- My hypothesis is that one of these 'boundary predators' had inserted its silver tube into the energy body of its prey for feeding, when its terminal became fixed within the body of its prey, linking them together ... This led to a form of trans-dimensional symbiosis and the establishment of an organism with both physical and "spiritual" (i.e. qi based) components.

- With further evolution of the neural complexity of the physical organism, the silver tube later extended throughout the body of its metazoan "prey" (or now, symbiont) as "energy meridians." Further replication of chakras at key points in the physical body now occurs, with specialization to allow access to different realms for energy/information inflows.

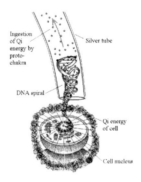

The final result of this hypothetical series of events is that spiritual beings from the energetic plane may now use the silver tube to enter a physical body on our plane through the centre of the chakra. Thus they come into intimate contact with the physical organisms they come to inhabit. They (and in my book I refer to these energetic beings as "we"), may also use this route to access astral or other planes, and to interrogate information stored in the Implicate Order.

Differentiation of the human chakras

A further speculation on the much later evolution of chakras seems to follow from the vertical posture adopted by our species and their ancestors over the last million years or so. Apart from the conventional theory that by rising on our hind legs we can more easily manipulate objects, or that this leads to reduced heat exposure on the savannah, the effect of attaining a vertical posture may also be reflected in the differentiation of the functions of our upper and lower chakras. Although I have not investigated this aspect, animals are said to have small or closed chakras. Through assuming a vertical posture, the crown chakra comes closer to the sky than the basal chakra, with the others in intermediate positions. Would it be strange therefore that the upper chakras become specialized for more ethereal communications and high frequency messages (the purple end of the spectrum—and the color usually assigned to the upper chakras), while earthly bodily functions (and their red coloration) are mediated by the lower chakras?

Conclusion

So what is the purpose of this series of speculations? Simply to illustrate that if the esoteric traditions view human beings as creatures capable (largely unconsciously) of time travel and movement between different dimensions, we should consider what possible mechanisms might have given rise to these possibilities in an evolutionary universe. By taking seriously the paranormal capabilities now established by investigators operating in the science tradition, and the huge body of traditional experience accumulated by "energy schools," we arrive at a state of mind where such speculations are natural outgrowths of both science and spirituality. One thing is certain: if your personal experience convinces you that a phenomenon is real, it is natural to enquire as to its possible origin, using those clues that are to hand.

References

Caddy, J.F. (2006). *A Return to Subjectivity*. Trafford Press.

Freke, T. and P.Gandy. (1989). *The Hermetica—The lost wisdom of the Pharaohs*. Tarcher/Putnam books.

Harner, M. (1982). *Way of the Shaman: A Guide to Power and Healing*. Bantam Books.

Jwing-Ming, Y. (1989). *Muscle/Tendon Changing and Marrow/Brain Wash-*

ing Chi Kung. YMAA Publication Center, Jamaica Plain, Massachussetts, USA.

Mandelbrot, B.B. (1983). *The Fractal Geometry of Nature.* W.H. Freeman and Co. NY.

Motoyama, H. (1995). *Theories of the Chakras.* Quest Books.

Pearson, H. (2003). "Beyond the double helix," *Nature* Vol 421, p 310-12.

Peitgen, H. and P. Richter (1986). *The Beauty of Fractals.* Springer-Verlag, Berlin.

Schnieider, E.D. and J.J. Kay (1994). "Complexity and thermodynamics: towards a new ecology," *Futures* 24, pp 624-647.

John F. Caddy *is a scientist with broad interests in dowsing, the paranormal, and shamanic activities, who has been engaged in personal investigations on qi phenomena as described in his recent book* A Return to Subjectivity, *published by Trafford press.*

The Continuing Strange Tale
of the Thylacine:
A Growth Function for
a Small Population
By Chris Payne

Introduction

Cryptozoologists are romantics. They spend their lives dreaming of lost or hidden animals that have somehow managed to remain out of sight in remote corners of our over-populated world. Expeditions are mounted to search out species that sometimes only exist in the oral histories of indigenous peoples, such as the attempts to locate the fabled *Orang pendek*, a small hominid supposedly living deep in the rain forests of Indonesia. And many people remain convinced that there exists a gigantic ape-like creature, known variously as the *Yeti* or *Sasquatch*, at high altitudes in east Asia and northwest America. Fortunes must have been spent searching for the Loch Ness Monster, which cryptozoologists still look for in spite of all the evidence that "sightings" of it have always been attributed to natural causes such as floating matter or the self-delusion of the observers. No amount of scientific persuasion seems to be enough to convince Nessie fans that a pod of pleisiosauri could not possibly survive in an enclosed area from the age of the dinosaurs.

However, large land animals previously unknown to regular zoologists do turn up from time to time. It was long believed that the okapi, discovered in 1930, would be the last large mammal to be discovered but since then other newcomers have been found. For example, as recently as the 1990s a group of mammals, previously unknown to western science, was discovered in Vietnam. These included a large bovid, the Vietnamese Ox or Saola, three species of small muntjac-like deer, and a civet. (Ref. 1) Such discoveries give heart to the cryptozoologists. They rightly point out that if an animal as large as an ox can stay hidden in the jungles of a densely-populated country like Vietnam, then who knows what other fauna still remain to be discovered? The cryptozoologist's bible is Bernard Heuvelmanns' famous, and very readable, book, *On the*

Track of Unknown Animals, (Ref. 2) a catalogue of marginal fauna. Published in 1958, almost all of its speculations remain unverified.

Undoubtedly though, it is quite possible that there exist small hidden remnant populations of animal species teetering between viability and extinction. Of all these, the continuing existence of a population of thylacine *(Thylacinus cynocephalus)* must be one of the most plausible. Officially declared extinct after the last known specimen was filmed shortly before its death in Hobart Zoo in 1936, the thylacine is, or at least was, a creature that is certainly not fictitious. Indeed, much is known about it since, if it became extinct, it did so within living memory. The official extinction declaration is regularly under informal challenge as sightings of the thylacine continue to be reported. The possibility of its continued existence was the subject of a paper by Evans 2004. (Ref. 3) As Evans points out, many of the sightings are unreliable and unscientific, but here and there a sighting is made by a reliable witness whose report cannot be dismissed as mere fancy, such as the famous Naarding sighting of 1982. On such evidence one must accept the possibility that the official declaration was premature, and there may indeed be a small population of thylacine living alive and well in the forests of Tasmania and, possibly, in Australia and Java as well. The population will necessarily be tiny or thylacines would be seen regularly. The animal certainly has much to fear from *Homo sapiens,* its principal enemy for the hundred and thirty years or so when the two species were in close contact–so it has every incentive to stay out of sight: its survival could only be in places remote from human beings. On the other hand, the thylacine has been much talked up by the residents of Tasmania who have every interest in the perpetuation of the thylacine legend. Like the villages around Loch Ness, Tasmania has developed a thriving cottage industry catering for tourists in search of a romantic mystery.

Evans' paper was an attempt to estimate the size of any thylacine population remaining in the wilds of Tasmania. Human beings have now stopped killing it for bounty so with its major predator no longer impeding its expansion, the species, if it exists, could recover. For tangible proof of its existence, there would need to be some concrete evidence in the form of a live capture or a dead specimen e.g. a road-kill, or at the very least an abundance of reliable sightings, photographs, or film. When, was Evans' question, would we be able to expect enough such evidence that the thylacine's existence could no longer be denied? Alternatively, by what year could we be sure, by a lack of such evidence, that the thylacine is truly extinct?

The Growth Model for the Population

Evans used Fibonnacci-like difference equations to test his hypothesis and, in an attempt to verify his analysis, we start from a similar point. A logical difference equation for population growth is:

$$F(n + 3) = p[F(n + 2) + F(n + 1) - F(n)] \qquad (1)$$

This model represents the real-life situation (certainly for human beings) where the birth of the great-grandchild occurs at or about the same time as the death of the great-grandparent. The factor p expresses a generation-on-generation proportionate increase in the population which is necessary if the population is to grow. The range of p is > 1 for growth: p = 1 for a constant population model and p < 1 for population decline.

We can change the discrete n-values in equation (1) to a continuous variable x and replace differences by their approximate derivative equivalents using the well-known formulae with step increment = 1:

$$F(n + 3) \approx f_0''' + 3.f_0'' + 3.f_0' + f_0$$
$$F(n + 2) \approx f_0'' + 2.f_0' + f_0$$
$$F(n + 1) \approx f_0' + f_0$$
$$F(n) \approx f_0 \qquad (2)$$

where the prime denotes differentiation with respect to x and the subscript 0 implies the value at x = n. The variable x represents the generation value from some start point. These equations are approximate but the errors are ignored for what is an approximate speculative analysis.

Substitution of the relationships (2) into the difference equation (1), and dropping the subscripts will yield the following third-order differential equation.

$$f'''(x) + a.f''(x) + b.f'(x) + c.f(x) = 0 \qquad (3)$$

where $a = 3 - p$; $b = 3(1 - p)$ and $c = 1 - p$.

The standard solution method is by setting

$$f(x) = \lambda e^{mx} \qquad (4)$$

where l and m are constants. Substitution of equation (4) into the differential equation (3) will yield the cubic auxiliary equation after cancellation of λe^{mx}:

$$m^3 + a.m^2 + b.m + c = 0 \tag{5}$$

These days there is no shortage of graphical or numerical methods for the solution of a cubic equation but algebraic methods are needed if one is looking for an explicit solution. Of course, one could always use some clever modern algebraic software such as Mathematica™ to obtain the symbolic form of the roots, but I feel it is somehow "cheating", and not reliable, simply to push numbers into a computer program and get the answers as if by magic. A number of conventional methods exist for the solution of a cubic polynomial with real coefficients: we can use the oldest, Cardano's method. (See e.g. Ref 4)

First make the substitution $m=z-a/3$ in equation (5) to obtain the so-called *depressed cubic* without a term containing the square of the variable.

$$z^3 + z \left[b - \frac{a^2}{3} \right] + \left[\frac{2a^3}{27} - \frac{ba}{3} + c \right] = 0 \tag{6}$$

There is then a further substitution of the variable i.e.

$$z = u + \frac{a^2/a - b/3}{u} \tag{7}$$

so that

$$u^3 + \frac{[a^2/9 - b/3]^3}{u^3} + [2a^3/27 - ba/3 + c] = 0 \tag{8}$$

Multiplication of this equation by u3 will produce a sixth-degree polynomial which is really a quadratic equation in u^3.

$$u^6 + [2a^3/27 - ba/3 + c].u^3 + [a^2/9 - b/3]^3 = 0 \tag{9}$$

or, more simply

$$u^6 + Bu^3 + C = 0 \tag{10}$$

Where B=$[2a^3/27-ab/3+c]$ and C = $[a^2/9 - b/3]^3$ which is solved using the famous formula.

$$u^3 = \frac{-B \pm \sqrt{(B^2 - 4c)}}{2} \qquad (11)$$

Equation (11) can be solved using De Moivre's theorem and will have six complex solutions in three equal pairs which correspond to three cube roots of u. The solution for m which follows by back substitution exists in three regions.

For p<1, the solution form consists of a single real root and a complex pair; p=1, there is a trivial solution { -2, 0, 0 }; p>1, the solution has three real roots.

Ignoring the trivial case, the solutions for f(x), the growth function, can be written

$$f(x) = K(p)exp[m_1(p)x] + exp[real\ (m_2(p))x]$$
$$\{L(p).cos(imag(m_2(p)).x)$$
$$+M(p).sin(imag(m_2(p)).x)\} \quad p<1 \qquad (12)$$

$$f(x) = K(p)exp[m_1\ (p).x] + L(p)exp[m_2(p).x] + M(p)exp[m_3(p).x] \quad p>1$$

where K,L,M are the unknown coefficients. The three real roots are numbered 1, 2, 3 and the parts of the complex roots for the p <1 solution are realm2 and imagm2. K, L and M are functions of p, to be determined from the boundary conditions.

$f(0) = R$; $f(1) = R.p$ and $f(2) = R.p^2$ where R is the size of the original remnant population.

It would be possible to write equation (12), the growth function, as an explicit relationship f = f(x,p,R), but the algebra is formidably heavy, so this is the point at which we resort to modern technology in the form of a spreadsheet. A sensible range of values for p where p>1 would be 1.01(0.01)1.15 i.e. a generational growth rate range between 1% and 15%. The solution table is Table 1.

It is immediately seen that the term $M(p).exp[m_3(p).x]$ makes little contribution to growth rates and can be discarded. Thus the growth function can be rewritten

$$f(x) = K(p).\ exp[m_1(p)x] + L(p).exp[m_2(p)x] \quad p>1 \qquad (13)$$

Each of the functions K(p), L(p), $m_1(p)$ and $m_2(p)$ can be replaced by continuous functions derived via a difference table. The following are good approximations.

$K(p) = R.\{0.86p^2 - 2.35p + 1.96\}$

$M_1(p) = 23.18p^3 - 79.52p^2 + 92.64 - 36.24$ (14)

$L(p) R.\{1.45p - 0.95\}$

$m_2(p) = 0.75 - 0.82\,p$

For the region p<1, a single value of p will suffice to demonstrate that the population will decline. Putting p = 0.99, the growth function becomes

$$f(x)R.\{0.0067e^{-1.9975x} + e^{-0.0063x}[0.9946\cos(0.0705x) - 0.205\sin(0.0705x)]\}\ (15)$$

which goes to f(x) = 0 after about 20 generations.

P	K/R	m_1	L/R	m_2	M/R	m_3
1.01	0.4918	0.0722	0.5144	-0.0647	-0.0062	-2.0025
1.02	0.4597	0.1131	0.5539	-0.0882	-0.0136	-2.0025
1.03	0.4511	0.1424	0.5693	-0.1050	-0.0204	-2.0074
1.04	0.4442	0.1682	0.5832	-0.1184	-0.0274	-2.0098
1.05	0.4380	0.1918	0.5965	-0.1296	-0.0345	-2.0122
1.06	0.4326	0.2138	0.6091	-0.1393	-0.0416	-2.0146
1.07	0.4271	0.2348	0.6218	-0.1478	-0.0489	-2.0169
1.08	0.4222	0.2548	0.6340	-0.1555	-0.0563	-2.0192
1.09	0.4176	0.2740	0.6460	-0.1625	-0.0639	-2.0215
1.10	0.4130	0.2927	0.6582	-0.1688	-0.0712	-2.0238
1.11	0.4087	0.3108	0.6702	-0.1747	-0.0788	-2.0261
1.12	0.4045	0.3284	0.6820	-0.1801	-0.0865	-2.0283
1.13	0.4004	0.3457	0.6940	-0.1852	-0.0944	-2.0305
1.14	0.3962	0.3627	0.7061	-0.1899	-0.1023	-2.0327
1.15	0.3923	0.3793	0.7180	-0.1944	-0.1103	-2.0349

Table 1. Solution of the Growth Rate Function for p>1

Interpretation of Results

Like Evans, the implicit assumption is that year zero for the thylacine was 1936 and that only a few individuals had survived the bounty hunters who were not put out of business until the species had almost completely disappeared. Indeed, the last authenticated killing occurred in 1930 and hunting permits for thylacine were still being issued up until only two months before the death of the Hobart Zoo specimen and the extinction declaration. (Ref 5).

We can be fairly sure that a thylacine would probably live about 9 years in the wild given that the captive animal died when it was about 12. Predators in zoos do not have to catch their own food and as older wild animals lose their mobility they will starve to death. Prey also become too slow to evade their predators so a zoo can be viewed as a kind of life support system for geriatric animals who would not be able to survive in the wild. Based on a life span of nine years, the thylacine generation would be roughly a third of this, or three years. From year zero, fifteen generations take us to 1982 and the famous Naarding sighting: 24 generations brings us to 2008. Table 2 is drawn for values of R of 2, 5, 10 and 19 and for $p = 1.05$ and $p = 1.09$. The population sizes at years 1982, 2008, 2026 (30 generations from 1936) and 2036 (33 generations) are estimated.

In his paper Evans makes two assumptions. First he extrapolates that a single breeding pair in 1936 would have about 68 descendants today. This would imply a breeding rate of something like 1.05. The above model agrees well with Evans and gives an estimate of 87.

If the breeding rate is about 1.05 then Evans' other assumption will not hold. This was that the thylacine population of 1982 would be about 500 descended from a start population of 19. For that to be the case, the growth rate would need to be more like 1.09 (See Table 2). A start population of 19 and a growth rate of 1.09 would result in a present population of nearly 6000--a population large enough that the question of existence would already be closed.

Taking the value $p = 1.05$ and $R < 20$, then, if the thylacine exists, its present population will probably still be in the hundreds. If Evans is correct and 5000 individuals will be needed before there are regular sightings, then we might be able to expect an increasing rate of reliable reports from now on. However, the magical decisive 5000 will not be reached for many years yet, so the Tasmanian thylacine tourism industry still has some life left in it. If the status of the thylacine is still unchanged from what it is today by the mid 2030s then we can be sure the animal is truly extinct.

TABLE 2: PREDICTIONS OF THE THYLACINE
POPULATION AT DIFFERENT YEARS

The 5% Model

Year	R=2	R=5	R=10	R=19
1936	2	5	10	19
1982	16	39	79	149*
2008	87	218	436	828
2026	275	687	1375	2612
2036	489	1221	2443	4641

The 9% Model

Year	R=2	R=5	R=10	R=19
1936	2	5	10	19
1982	82	129	258	490*
2008	610	1525	3050	5794
2026	3170	7926	15852	30118
2036	7228	18071	36141	68668

* Year of the famous Naarding sighting

A Note on Cardano's Method for the Roots of a Cubic Polynomial

While I was thinking about this paper, a colleague, who is a graduate in mathematics from one of the top Ivy League American universities and who subsequently became a professor of history, asked me what I was doing. After I had told him, he replied that I would be using some graphical method for solution of my cubic auxiliary equation, there being no algebraic general method for the solution of a cubic! This led me to wonder how many other mathematics graduates have never heard of Cardano and the method which bears his name. I certainly never met it when I was an A-level student at grammar school in the 1950s and it did not appear on the University of London BSc General mathematics syllabus. It is entirely possible that generations of students have graduated in mathematics under the misapprehension that the only solutions for the roots of polynomials greater than degree 2 are by graph or software.

The method has an interesting history. It was one of the first independent achievements of Renaissance mathematics, something which had been unknown to the ancients. In Cardano's time, mathematicians, even the great Fermat, did not believe in negative numbers or their roots and when Cardano published the method in his *Ars Magna* of 1545, he referred to these unbelievable answers as "useless." In spite of this, he almost stumbled on the discovery of complex numbers at least a century or more before Argand and De Moivre.

Footnote

Girolamo Cardano (1501-1576) was an interesting character who lived an eventful and picaresque life. He was a bitter man with much to be bitter about. He began life as an illegitimate whose mother had tried to abort him. He suffered repeated rejection from the College of Physicians in Milan because of his aggressive outspokenness and he spent time in jail for heresy. There were the premature deaths of his sons, one a feckless ne'er-do-well, the other tortured and executed for murder. But his self-contained character was such that he cheerfully admitted to being an amoral, vindictive cheat. Even the method which bears his name is not really his. It was actually the discovery of his talented contemporary Nicolo Fontana Tartaglia (1500—1557). The story goes that Cardano persuaded Tartaglia to reveal his method to him after Cardano had sworn an oath that he would not publish it. True to form, Cardano broke his promise and included the method in Ars Magna. Surprisingly, given his character, he was gracious enough to attribute the work to Tartaglia thus avoiding adding academic plagiarism to his other achievements. There is an excellent online biography of Cardano by O'Connor and Robertson (Ref 6).

Acknowledgements

The author thanks Loida Suaco Payne for reading the proof and for helpful comments.

This paper is reprinted with permission from *Mathematics Today*, the Bulletin of the Institute of Mathematics and its Applications, August 2008.

References

1. *http://www.animalinfo.org/species/artiperi/pseunghe.htm*
2. Heuvelmanns, Bernard, *On the Track of Unknown Animals*, Pub. Rupert Hart-Davis, London 1958
3. Evans, C.W., *The Strange Tale of the Thylacine, Mathematics Today*, Pub. Institute of Mathematics and its Applications, April 2004 pp 70-72
4. *http://thesaurus.maths.org/mmkb/entry.html?action=entryById&id=566*
5. *http://www.messybeast.com/extinct/thylacine.htm*
6. O'Connor, J.J and Robertson,E.F.
   http://www-groups.dcs.st-and.ac.uk/~history/Biographies/Cardan.html

Chris Payne is a mathematician based at Girne American University, Kyrenia, Cyprus.

History, the Hive Mind, and Agrarian Art
by Mark Pilkington

Folkloric and fortean phenomena rarely emerge fully formed from a cultural vacuum; instead they occur at the meeting points of perceived experience, imagination, history, and culture. Sometimes, however, these phenomena do seem to evolve and develop of their own accord, maintaining for themselves a veneer of authenticity and plausibility by remaining relevant to their times. Regardless of what may actually lie at the roots of these events, stories, and experiences, in reality it is not the phenomena themselves that carry out this conservation work but the people who experience them, the people who write about them, and the people who read what is written about them. They serve as lines of transmission through which anomalous accounts can be generated, amplified, propagated, and mutated.

If we do grant some phenomena an autonomous existence, or at least the appearance of one, then we should be able to study their phylogeny as biologists study that of living and once-living things. But, just as there are crucial gaps and anomalies in the fossil record, so there are problems when trying to present a case for the smooth emergence and natural development of anomalies. We encounter particular difficulties when we try to assess historical reports. Can medieval records of unusual aerial phenomena be read in the same way as contemporary UFO reports? Are Native American accounts of bipedal manimals the equivalent of present day Bigfoot sightings? Are these objects, entities, and events part of a phenomenal continuum, or do our interpretative frameworks change so much across multiple cultures and centuries that our attempts to fit them into such a continuum become little more than well-intentioned solipsism?

In examining a relatively recent and well-documented phenomenon—crop circles—we can see how fraught with paradox attempts to historicize the anomalous can be.

The crop circle story appears to be largely cut and dried. Having spent some years as a member of a circlemaking team, my take on the formations themselves is, perhaps, unfortean: anything more complex than a shapeless blob has been made by humans. I can also personally attest to the fact that some shapeless blobs are made by humans too. End of discussion. Sorry! The reasons why some people refuse to accept this fact, and how these people respond to and are affected by the formations are, ultimately, more interesting and anomaly-rich than the question of their creation, but that is another question for another day.

Doug Bower and Dave Chorley began making crop circles in their native Hampshire, southern England, in the summer of 1976. Bower has often stated that the initial inspirations for their first circle were the peculiar and unexplained "saucer nests" found in marshy reeds around Queensland, Australia, which he read about while living in that country. One incident in particular made the Australian news. On 19 January 1966, farmer George Pedley saw a 25ft (8m) diameter, grey, saucer-shaped *something* rise, with a loud hissing sound, from reeds alongside a lagoon near Tully. The thing shot off into the skies at great speed, leaving behind it a flattened bed of swirled reeds. The media got hold of Pedley's story and images of the whorl of reeds made the national papers. Bower was already fascinated with UFOs and the story made a strong impression on him.

Back in the UK a decade later, one fateful night during the long, hot summer of 1976, Doug and Dave left the first of what would be a great many "UFO landing sites" in the fields of Southern England. The only problem was that it would be several years until anybody else noticed them. In fact Doug and Dave's crop circles didn't make their media debut until the *Wiltshire Times* ran an article on the "Mystery Circles" in August 1980. It would be almost another decade again before the circles became a national, then an international, obsession, and one that shows little sign of abating over thirty years later.

So far, this would seem to be a straightforward enough history. An apparently genuine anomaly inspires artists to create their own versions, opening a Pandora's box that, despite repeated explanations and revelations from the circlemakers themselves, refuses to be closed.

But it's not quite as simple as that. There are hiccups in this history. Glitches in the otherwise smooth process of ostension, the process by which fictional or folkloric events seep into living reality.

The famed "mowing devil" pamphlet of 1678 describes a neat circle mown into the field of an unscrupulous land owner, an act depicted as being the work of the Devil himself. Whether this account was intended to be read as a *bonafide* news report, as a cautionary parable, or both, it is difficult for us to say, but it is just one of many reports of strange goings on, portents, omens, and miracles during this troubled period of English history. Less well known, even within the croppie community, are Professor Robert Plot's illustrations from his *The Natural History of Staffordshire* (1686), showing curious geometric markings—circles, squares within circles, wavy lines—found on the ground.

These, Plot suggests, could have been produced by wind, lightning, meteors, or animals, while the local populace usually attributed them to demons or faeries... *plus ça change*... Accounts of rural lovers creating circular crop-beds as discrete venues for their amorous activities in the late 19th century have also emerged in recent years. It's extremely unlikely that Doug Bower and Dave Chorley knew anything about these historical antecedents to their work, but it shouldn't really surprise us that they weren't the first people to flatten a circular area of crop in a field.

Equally curious but far better documented is the occurrence, in the very public setting of a modestly-budgeted British-American science fiction film, of a crop formation that predates Doug and Dave's work by perhaps three years. The formation is also of a complexity that wouldn't be seen in the field for at least another 15 years.

While preparing *The Field Guide: The Art, History and Philosophy of Crop Circle Making* with authors and circlemakers Rob Irving and John Lundberg, I re-watched *Phase IV.* Released in the UK in 1973 and in the USA in 1974, the film had been a late-night TV favorite of my youth, but one that I hadn't seen for years.

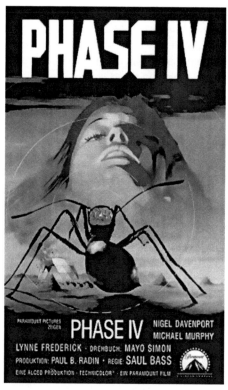

It's the first and last film to be directed by Saul Bass, who designed celebrated posters and title sequences for Alfred Hitchcock, Stanley Kubrick, Martin Scorsese, and others. Thoughtful, apocalyptic, psychedelic, and environmentally-aware, *Phase IV* is an intriguing entry into the cycle of dystopian, realist science fiction cinema represented by the likes of *The Andromeda Strain* (1971), *Silent Running* (1972), and *Soylent Green* (1973). It also shares a paranoid mindset with the hokier "revenge of nature" films that were popular at the time (e.g. *The Hellstrom Chronicle* [1971], using the same ant cinematographer, Ken Middleham, *Frogs* [1972], *Bug* [1975 - Middleham again] and *Food of the Gods* [1976]). *Phase IV*'s screenwriter, Mayo Simon wrote one more film, *Futureworld*, a sequel to the robots-run-amok classic *Westworld*, an episode of the TV series *The Man from Atlantis*, and then seems to have dropped off the radar, or at least off the Internet Movie Database.

Phase IV, then, can be considered something of a one off.

While some find *Phase IV* unnecessarily ponderous—it's no *Empire of the Ants*—it's actually one of the more remarkable SF films of the era. Ken Middleham's stunning microphotography of the ants going about their sinister business sits perfectly with Bass's own solarized '70s sci-fi aesthetic, overflowing with strange architectural forms (both human and insect), geodesic domes, huge computers, oceans of magnetic tape, and, of course, the obligatory atonal synthesizer score—by David Vorhaus of the English 1960s electronic group White Noise. Mayo Simon's screenplay takes some interesting and surprising turns while asking us to consider the fragility of our anthropocentric existence on Earth, climaxing with an oblique and cosmic *2001*-style ending.

There's not a great deal of plot to worry about. An unusual planetary alignment in our solar system, heralded by some as the end of the world, causes planet Earth to be exposed to anomalous electromagnetic fields. Initially it seems that nothing has happened, but entomologists begin to observe odd behavior in ants: different ant species, normally aggressive to one another, are joining forces and attacking larger animals, including humans. Soon the ants are destroying whole towns, gnawing through wooden structures, and destroying crops and livestock. In an attempt to find out what is going on, a noted English entomologist, Dr Ernest Hubbs (Nigel Davenport), and a game theorist and mathematician, James Lesko (Michael Murphy), set out to observe a colony of the super-intelligent ants from the apparent safety of a geodesic biosphere in Arizona. Beforehand they visit a small family-run farm that has been attacked by the ants. And that's where we come in...

The two scientists enter a tall grass field to study a dead sheep. Two puncture marks are noted on its neck. Besides that there are no other signs of injury, but the crop has been mown into a strange geometric form, an upright square within a larger, cropped circle. Or should that be crop circle...?

So there we have it: a large-scale (perhaps 250 feet [84 metres] in diameter) pictogram in a science fiction film that few people have seen and that was released some three years before Doug and Dave set to work in England. What's more, the crop circle is decorated with a classically-mutilated sheep, drained of blood and dumped in the middle of a field.

Such animal mutilations would become associated—rightly or wrongly—with crop circles by the early 1990s. A white horse that died a natural death near a large formation in Wiltshire in July 1990 may have been mutilated after its death, according to police, though some within the croppie community immediately raised the spectre of the 1970s American animal mutilation wave. That panic was in full effect while *Phase IV* was being shot and was presumably not unknown to the film-makers. Whether other animals that were later found in English crop formations (allegedly including birds and a sheep) were left there by the circlemakers or just happened to die nearby we can't know for sure. Perhaps some of the circlemakers saw *Phase IV* on video, or on one of its late night TV appearances in 1984, 1993, and 1995? We can only specu-late, though the circlemakers are just as likely to have come up with the idea independently, if indeed they were responsible for the appearance of the dead animals in the first place.

Adding to the intrigue, one of the wind-blown crop glyphs portrayed in Robert Plot's T*he Natural History of Staffordshire*, a square within a circle, is identical to the one in *Phase IV*. It would be extremely surpris-ing if any of the film-makers had ever seen Plot's obscure tome, though the square within the circle is hardly a new geometric concept.

Might Doug or Dave have seen *Phase IV*, and been influenced by it? Doug's memory isn't what it might once have been, but he doesn't recall seeing it, and Dave is no longer with us. As a self-confessed UFO buff, it's possible that Doug may have seen the film on its release. But if one of them did see it, why didn't they borrow more from the film? Doug and Dave didn't introduce right angles into their work until 1990, when they were inspired to do so by a 1915 painting by Georges Ribemont-Dessaignes. By using straight lines the duo sought to demonstrate that the formations couldn't possibly have been made by Terrence Meaden's "plasma vortices", the favoured scientific explanation of the day. Such pictograms, as they became known, were taken a stage further by the younger, second wave of circlemakers, who appeared on the scene with their iconic key-shaped glyphs, triangles and what were known as insec-tograms. At which point we have come full circle.

It's interesting that the *Phase IV* formation is presented as a message of some kind—this is never really explained, though the ants do commu-nicate with the scientists using simple geometric forms later in the film.

Again, if the film was an influence on Doug and Dave wouldn't they also have borrowed the idea of the symbols as interspecies communications? Initially they wanted only to create UFO landing sites. It was only much later, in the early 1990s, that the crop formations were regarded by their audience as signals from aliens/Mother Earth/the secret government/etc. and were then shaped by the circlemakers to fulfill that diplomatic role.

So what do we have here? A small mystery-within-a-mystery; a meta-fortean occurrence; further evidence, as if it was needed, that all our futures will one day become yesterday's science fiction. Certainly the *Phase IV*-mation represents a fine example of ostension—we might call it *precognitive* ostension—and one without a clear channel of transmission into the real world of crop circles. It reminds us that the veil between reality and fantasy remains wisp thin and continuously porous, and that we might at any time cross its boundaries without ever being aware of it. When you are dealing with the anomalous, even when it is of mundane provenance like the crop circles, you should not be surprised to find anomalies creeping into your existence. Like attracts like; strangeness attracts strangeness.

This affair also begs those immortal questions: where do ideas come from, and where do they go once they've been thought up? Are ideas our own or are they merely a property, or a side effect, of the conscious universe, the hive mind? Perhaps we might consider, in the manner of J.W. Dunne's 1921 *An Experiment with Time,* that when we leave the realm of physical objects and enter that of information and consciousness, the flow of time might not always be in a single direction. Ideas from the past might drift into the future—or vice versa—without a tangible line of transference and without requiring witnesses, reporters, theories, blurry photographs, or any of the other traditional stepping stones of anomalous investigation.

But that's enough speculation for now; we've crossed the fence and entered another, stranger field, and the ants are calling us to return.

Mark Pilkington runs Strange Attractor Press and has published three Strange Attractor Journal anthologies, The Field Guide, Welcome to Mars, and Medical London. Far Out, an anthology of his weird science columns for the Guardian newspaper is available from Disinformation books. His book Mirage Men, about the intelligence agencies' exploitation on UFO lore, will be published by Constable Robinson in 2010. Phase IV is now available on DVD.

Some Deleted Notes to
Politics and the Occult: The Left, the Right, and the Radically Unseen
By Gary Lachman

The following are some notes that for space considerations had to be deleted from my book *Politics and the Occult: The Left, the Right, and the Radically Unseen*, published in the fall of 2008 by Quest Books in the United States. Like most writers, I'm loathe to cut anything once I've completed a book, but given that I had already exceeded the word limit in the main text, I conceded to the publisher's request that I jettison the long and, to me at least, elucidating additional material that accompanied some sections of the book.

I was unhappy doing this, as I felt that the notes did add to the main narrative. Yet it also seemed that when I tried to incorporate them into the text, the "flow"—that mysterious forward drive all writers seek to capture—shifted, and the pace of the narrative slowed. C.S. Lewis said somewhere that a writer's job is to keep the narrative going in one direction and avoid getting caught in eddies and drifts that collect along the sides—or something like that. Deferring to this wisdom, and my publisher's demands, I cut the material. Yet it seemed too interesting to discard. Hence the rather unusual idea of submitting it to *The Anomalist*. I imagine that in one sense this is actually appropriate, for where else could we find such an anomaly as publishing the notes to several sections of a book, without the book itself?

As the title suggests, the notes all deal with the theme of politics and the occult. I first thought to include the parts of the book the notes relate to, but it struck me that this would perhaps create more confusion than not, and, aside from some alterations in structure, the notes were, in some sense, self-contained, and could be expanded into individual essays. It's either evidence of my laziness, or of a wish to gamble with the risk of their appearing incomprehensible, that I've left them as they are, and have merely added a brief indication of the topic to which they refer. An enterprising reader with nothing better to do and the good sense to

POLITICS AND THE OCCULT

purchase a copy of *Politics and the Occult*, could try to find their original home. There's no prize offered, but I'd be interested to see if anyone can follow the editing trail to the source.

On the problem of egalitarianism and "higher types"

In his last years the great humanist psychologist Abraham Maslow became troubled by the political implications of his psychology of "self-actualization." Among other ideas, this entailed a concept of being "fully human," which suggested that, in Maslow's uncomfortable phrase, "some people are more 'human' than others." Maslow wrote that "the problem of the 'biological elite' has inescapably confronted me in my efforts to build a theory of the good society." By the "biological elite" Maslow meant "self-actualizing" men and women, individuals who, for one reason or another, "actualize" their potential, and, as result of this, experience a greater degree of psychological health than those who do not, evidence for this being the repeated recurrence of "peak experiences," moments of an almost mystical sense of happiness and fulfillment. What sets "self-actualizers" apart from less psychologically healthy people—everyone from psychopaths to the merely discontented and neurotic—was, Maslow concluded, some innate, biological disposition, something, that is, *inside* them. To be sure, social and economic conditions can help or hinder one's "actualization." But as Maslow points out, many of the "self-actualizers" he studied came from deprived backgrounds and made real their potentials *in spite of* adverse conditions. (In fact, in some cases, difficult conditions may even be a spur to "self-actualization.") Maslow envisioned a time "when there is no longer social injustice to serve as an alibi or excuse for one's own biological inadequacies" and when there "might well be a great increase of [...] malicious envy of those who are more successful in their achievements."

Thinking of ways to "protect the biologically gifted from the almost inevitable malice of the biologically non-gifted," Maslow suggested something like a new "priestly class to which is given less monetary reward and fewer privileges or luxuries than the average members of the overall population," given that "self-actualizers" are less interested in material rewards than in the "metagratifications" or "intrinsic values" of "advancing beauty, excellence, justice or truth."

Maslow's vision of a kind of Brahmin caste of "self-actualizers," uninterested in the kind of material gratification that most people desire and oriented toward more "spiritual" concerns, is a recurring fantasy in the world of occult politics. It's the basis for Hermann Hesse's monumental novel *The Glass Bead Game*, in which, in some unspecified future, a society of philosophers, artists, and other "gifted" individuals form a cultural elite, set apart from the masses. In the 1920s, in a book called *The Art of Being Ruled*, the British painter and novelist Wyndham Lewis, a writer not usually associated with anything even vaguely occult, suggested essentially the same arrangement as Maslow. Lewis argued that with the rise of democracy and egalitarianism, cultural values were increasingly being leveled and that mediocrity was becoming the norm, something we experience today as "dumbing down." One result of this is that the intellectuals considered the average person a "yahoo"— from Swift's *Gulliver's Travels*—and the ordinary man saw the artist as some sort of freak. To safeguard high cultural values and to maintain social order, Lewis argued that society should be split into two classes. Instead of the old, inequitable chasm between the "haves" and the "have-nots"—in which a small group of people get to do the things that most of the others want to do too—there would be "something like a *biological* separating-out of the chaff from the grain," the "chaff" being the person motivated by material desires and entertainments, the "grain" being the philosopher or artist—or, in Maslow's term, the "self-actualizer." (See Abraham Maslow "Humanistic Biology: Elitist Implications of the Concept of 'Full-Humanness'" in *Future Visions: The Unpublished Papers of Abraham Maslow*, ed. Edward Hoffman, Sage Publications: Thousand Oaks, 1996.)

The reader will note that this is among Maslow's *unpublished* works, suggesting that he was aware of the difficulty in discussing such inflammatory issues, especially at the time he wrote it, in 1968, when the notions of what we call "political correctness" were first taking root. Today, although biological and evolutionary psychology are established disciplines, the difficulty in airing any doubts about the dictums of egalitarianism remain and, indeed, have only increased. About another paper, on the "failure" of liberalism, Maslow's editor Hoffman remarks that it showed Maslow "slowing moving toward a stance that today would be most closely associated with neo-conservatism." (p. 160) That Maslow was also fond of the work of the novelist Ayn Rand, an outspoken advocate of capitalism and a critic of the welfare state, highlights the complexities of "spiritual politics." Maslow was one of the major figures associated with the Esalen Institute, the famous West Coast counter-culture "think tank" whose ethos was as far removed from Ayn Rand's as possible, and whose lack of intellectual rigor eventually led Maslow to reject its approach. Self-motivation, personal responsibility, and self-discipline—character traits of Maslow's "self-actualizers"—have much in common with the "rugged individualism" associated with the heroes of Rand's novels, and which was under attack in the 1960s and '70s by a variety of "alternative" schools of thought, from the New Left to feminists.

On Rousseau's dictum that we are "born free" but are subsequently "chained" by civilization

Some years ago the singer Bob Dylan posed an interesting question: "If dogs run free, why can't we?" The answer to this is that dogs *don't* run free. Dogs, like other non-human animals, are laden with the chains of their biology and are hemmed in by systems of instinct they are unable to throw off. Because dogs aren't expected to conform to the requirements of civilized behavior, they can engage in activities that to us *seem* free but really aren't. No dog can choose to react to a stimulus or not, in the way that we can. (And whether or not we do is a different question.) Disappointing as it may seem for those who hold sentimental and romantic views about animals, the most harried nine-to-fiver is *categorically* freer than any dog. What romantics like Dylan envy about dogs and other animals is not their freedom, which is severely limited, but their *unselfconsciousness*, their lack of an ego and its often debilitating concerns. The plunge into a supposed "animal-consciousness" sought by some is motivated by a desire to escape the human birth right of self-consciousness, which, while often a burden, can be, when brought to its proper state, something much freer than any animal can ever experience.

On popular culture, "freedom," and the right to be stupid, in the context of the musical criticism of the neo-Marxist Theodore Adorno and the esoteric fascist Julius Evola

It should be pointed out that the "jazz" both Adorno and Evola are talking about is not, say, that of a John Coltrane, but more along the lines of the Tin Pan Alley of the 1920s and the '30s Big Band sound. No doubt rock music would have raised their respective ire as would more recently rap. Which is not to say that because both Adorno and Evola can be criticized for "going over the top" in their reaction to jazz (or in what we can assume their reaction to more recent popular music would have been), that they were necessarily wrong to criticize it or other elements of popular culture. Although both can appear heavily authoritarian and intolerant, a great deal of what we all popular culture warrants the kind of censure Evola and Adorno gave it. In many ways, the rise of popular culture can be seen as a kind of microcosm of modern and post-modern political debate. Television, for example, and especially so-called reality-TV, is not known to be a particularly challenging form of entertainment, and in the eyes of some cultural critics, is little more than an agent of "dumbing-down." Yet it's extremely popular. Again, fast foods are known to be nutritionally lacking, to add to environmental problems, and to promote ill-health, yet they too are extremely popular. Health and a high level of culture are considered desirable aims. Yet personal freedom, the liberty to choose what to eat, and what to entertain oneself with is an equally desirable good. But when one's personal freedom manifests in sitting on a couch eating junk food while watching television for hours on end, it's difficult to avoid the sense that this is an abuse of that freedom. Yet the alternative, with the state *compelling* its citizens to be healthy and to interest themselves in something more profitable than television, seems equally abusive. The choice seems to be between having the freedom to be stupid, fat, and unhealthy, and having what in the UK is called a "nanny state," with the government, *for your own good*, keeping you in line at every step. Naturally, this situation wouldn't arise if people disciplined themselves and limited their intake of junk food and television, or for that matter, went without them at all; but the number of people capable of and willing to engage in this self-discipline has always been low, and they have always formed a minority. Some may argue that people *really* do want to eat well and to enjoy higher forms of entertainment, but they are manipulated by those that profit from junk food and TV to become addicted to these. Personally, I find that difficult to believe, especially given that no one forces anyone to choose a Big Mac rather than a salad, or to watch *Big Brother* rather than read Orwell. The choice remains up to me. It was the great hope of the 19th century that through education, the "masses" could be raised out of the cultural gutter and brought to appreciate the finer things. Now, if one were to argue something similar, charges of "political incorrectness" would be swift in coming, and the whole idea would be labeled "fascist." "Freedom" has in many ways become associated with being ignorant and lazy, and the idea that one should "improve" oneself is seen as "elitist" and "authoritarian." If it really is the case that people really want junk food and bad television, then, in a democratic state, those who argue that they shouldn't, are in the minority, and must abide by the decision of the majority. Which raises the question of which is more important: having the "freedom" to choose, or that which in fact you *actually do* choose. Is the "right to be stupid" more important than the "responsibility to be intelligent"? In such a state, government would ensure that the majority were left alone to enjoy living as they do, without interference by the few who desire something more than this. Thus from a consideration of popular culture, we arrive at different views of human nature.

On forms of political "gnosis"

Adorno's sources for the emancipation of society from the clutches of "late-capitalism"—a particular form of René Guenon's "reign of quantity"—tend to be the priesthood of "high modernism," the music of Arnold Schoenberg or the writings of Samuel Becket, whose "difficult," we might even say "esoteric" character, prevents them from being absorbed by the "low-brow" "culture industry" and allows them to retain a "revolutionary" power. Yet the effect is the same: a small group of "Gnostics"—those "in the know"—who work to influence the wider public. And indeed, in the radical days of the 1960s, when the work of Herbert Marcuse, with Adorno a member of the Frankfurt School, was immensely (and ironically) popular, the "revolutionary elite" among college students, inspired by Marcuse's and Adorno's critiques of bourgeois society, put into practice some of these ideals—although, more often than not, the soundtrack was by Jimi Hendrix and not Schoenberg, with a text by Hesse and not Beckett.

Mention of "Gnostics" brings to mind another oddly "occult" aspect of the Left's critique of modernity. In works like Adorno's *Negative Dialectics* and others, society in the grip of late capitalism is often depicted as such a total state of affairs, with practically nothing escaping its control, that it frequently resembles the Gnostic description of the material world in the hands of the evil Archons. In Gnostic mythology, the world was created by a kind of false God, an idiot demi-urge, and is under constant surveillance by dark spirits called Archons, a situation exploited cinematically with great success in the films like *The Matrix* and its sequels. Reading neo-Marxist descriptions of life under late capitalism, when *everything* is tainted by its techniques of control, and in which all attempts at escape lead back into the system, it's difficult not to see a parallel with the bleak, depressing, and angst-ridden world view of the Gnostics for whom the entire creation was a cosmic trap, an ontological version of Max Weber's "iron cage." A similar sense of things regarding the modern world led radicals, both of the Left and the Right, to do the one thing remaining, to try to smash as much of the cage as possible, with, as can be imagined, often tragic results.

On modern "ludibriums," or "serious jokes,"
a literary genre apparently put to great use by the authors
of the notorious "Rosicrucian manifestoes" of the early 1600s

Although the parallels may not seem immediately apparent, I submit that one example of an occult *ludibrium* in modern times may be that mind-numbing work of esoteric loquacity, *Beelzebub's Tales to His Grandson*, by G.I. Gurdjieff, a work whose difficulty is legendary. Although undoubtedly stuffed with valuable insights, in order to arrive at the nuggets of spiritual nutrition in this jaw-breaking text, one must chew through layers of esoteric leg-pulling. Not all devotees of this work have, in my opinion, succeeded in differentiating between the serious bits and the jokes, and it is difficult at times not to arrive at the conclusion that Gurdjieff himself was not always certain which was which.

On the political philosopher Leo Strauss' idea of 'esoteric writing,"
texts designed to avoid the censor and to "stagger"
the impact of "dangerous" ideas

Such Straussian ideas may be behind the notorious difficulty characteristic of much esoteric (in the occult sense) writing. Again, Gurdjieff's *Beelzebub's Tales to His Grandson* immediately springs to mind. Another, in a different way, is Rudolf Steiner's early epistemological work *The Philosophy of Freedom*, a careful reading of which forces the reader to participate in the kind of mental activity the work describes. This notion can be applied to other works as well, with the caveat that mere obscurity and difficulty should not be uniformly taken as a sign that profundity lies within. Some works are simply badly written and have little to communicate.

On the idea that "hidden forces" are behind everyday politics
and that human beings are merely the conduits
through which spiritual agencies work

It's curious that a very similar idea was promoted in recent decades, not by theocrats, but by believers in the power of "social forces" to rule and determine our lives. The idea, presented in different ways by thinkers like Michel Foucault, Jacques Derrida, and others is that the individual is *really* only a conduit for a variety of supremely powerful—but often obscure—"forces," like language (Derrida) or "discourse" (Foucault), over which we have no control and which, whether we like it or not, govern our lives and even our thoughts. In some extreme versions, the very desire to rebel is merely another expression of the powers that prompt it. Oddly, both Foucault and Derrida's nihilistic philosophies share with some radical religious views, such as those of the Traditionalists, a profoundly pessimistic anti-humanism. Both reject the idea that the majority of people have any control over their lives or even want any, and both see the kind of democracy associated with the west as an illusion destined to fade out in the near future.

On Julius Evola's racist, pro-Teutonic and
pro-militarist reading of Nietzsche

Evola's relationship with Nietzsche is fraught with irony. As pointed out earlier, Nietzsche scorned racism and had no sympathy for anti-Semitism. He was also anti-militarist, his celebration of the "good war that hallows any cause" being taken out of context on more than one occasion. Nietzsche also had no interest in the kind of Nordic, Teutonic ethos that excited Evola. Like Goethe, Hölderlin, Hesse, and other German poets, Nietzsche's vision was *southern*: he sang the praises of the Mediterranean, the area of Europe that Evola castigated as "promiscuous" and "lunar." In order to wash his ears of his once-beloved Wagner (the Nordic composer par excellence), Nietzsche claimed to have listened to Bizet's *Carmen* dozens of times. Although Nietzsche was appropriated by the Nazis, he would have had nothing but contempt for them. To be sure, Evola argues that Nietzsche "lacks Tradition," but then Nietzsche would not have been bothered by this.

On the shared pessimism of Adorno and Evola

Curiously, although he was castigated by 1960s student radicals for not being radical enough, Theodor Adorno's neo-Marxist aphoristic work *Minima Moralia* shares with Evola's last book, *Ride the Tiger* (a right wing *Rough Guide* to enduring modernity) a certain air of resignation, and a sense that there is no escape from the predicament, which, for both Evola and Adorno is the modern world—in Adorno's case because it is encased in the shell of "late capitalism." Both exhibit a kind of desperation, and both see the trap as seamless. For Adorno, "The whole is the false," and there is nothing for philosophy to do except to attempt to perceive all things as they would look in the light of an impossible redemption. *Minima Moralia* (Verso: London, 1984) pp. 50, 247.

Gary Lachman is the author of several books on the connected themes of consciousness and the counterculture, most recently Politics and the Occult: The Left, The Right, and The Radically Unseen *(Quest*

Books 2008). A revised and updated edition of his Turn Off Your Mind, *a history of the occult roots of the 1960s counterculture, will be published by Dedalus Books in late 2009 as* The Dedalus Book of the 1960s: Turn Off Your Mind. *He is a regular contributor to* The Independent on Sunday, Fortean Times, *and other journals, and is a frequent broadcaster on* BBC Radio 3.

EXPLORATIONS INTO THE MIND OF THE MAGICIAN: SÉANCES, MIND DOCTORS, AND THE FIRST FILM OF A CONJUROR BY RICHARD WISEMAN

When I was eight years old, I saw something that changed my life. My grandfather handed me a marker pen and asked me to write my initials on a coin. He carefully placed the coin on his palm and closed his hand. After gently blowing on his fingers, he opened his hand, and the coin had mysteriously vanished. Next, he reached into his pocket and took out a small tin box that was sealed with several elastic bands. My grandfather handed me this rather strange-looking package and asked me to remove the elastic bands and open the box. The box contained a small red velvet bag. I carefully removed it, peeked inside, and couldn't believe my eyes. The bag contained the initialed coin.

My grandfather's magic trick sparked a fascination with conjuring that has lasted throughout my life. In my teens I became one of the youngest members of a world-famous magic club, The Magic Circle. In my twenties, I worked as a professional magician, performing card tricks at some of London's most fashionable West End restaurants. Once in a while, I even made an initialed coin disappear and reappear in a little cloth bag sealed in a small tin box. Deceiving people on a twice-nightly basis sparked a strong sense of curiosity about why people are fooled. That interest acted as the catalyst for a psychology degree and so initiated my career as an experimental psychologist.

Over the years, a handful of scientists (including my good self) have investigated the psychology of the magician, examining how these mind masters manipulate the attention, perception, and memory of others. In this article I am going to describe three of these investigations, looking at the psychology of the séance room, the work of the remarkable Joseph Jastrow, and my adventures uncovering the first ever film of a conjuror.

Suggestion in the séance room

Over the years, I have been involved in several projects exploring the psychology of magical and pseudo-psychic deception. One of my first set of studies examined the role of suggestion in the séance room. Much of this work was carried out with a friend of mine, Andy Nyman. Andy is a skilled actor and magician and helps create material for the highly successful British television illusionist, Derren Brown. I first met Andy many years ago at a conference on magic, and we discovered that we were both interested in the techniques used by fraudulent mediums in the nineteenth century to fake ghostly phenomena in the séance room. We were curious to discover whether the hundred-year-old techniques would still fool a modern-day audience and so decided to stage a series of unusual experiments.

The plan was simple. We would invite groups of people to attend a theatrical reconstruction of a Victorian séance and use various techniques, including suggestion, to fake spirit activity. We would then ask them to tell us what they had experienced so that we could assess whether they had been fooled by our attempts at deception.

First we needed a spooky-looking venue. We came across the House of Detention —a dark, dank, disused, underground Victorian prison in the heart of London. It was perfect. The owners kindly allowed us to hire this uninviting venue for a week, and we staged two fake shows per evening, with twenty-five people attending each séance.

When people arrived, they were asked to complete a short form asking them whether they believed in the existence of genuine paranormal phenomena. I then led the group through the maze of underground prison corridors, briefly relating the history of the Victorian séance. Eventually they were taken along a narrow ventilation shaft into a large room at the heart of the prison. Here Andy introduced himself to the group and explained that he would be playing the part of the medium for the evening. Lit only by candlelight, he asked everyone to join him around a large table in the center of the room.

For the next twenty minutes, Andy told the group a fictitious ghost story concerning the murder of a non-existent Victorian music-hall singer named Marie Ambrose. According to Andy's carefully crafted script, Marie had lived close to the prison, and her ghost had often been seen in the building. Andy then passed various objects around the group that were allegedly associated with her life, including a maraca, a handbell, and a wicker ball. In reality, I had bought the objects from a local junk shop a few days before the shows. All of the objects, and the table around which everyone was seated, had small spots of luminous paint on them so that the group would be able to see them in the dark. Andy placed the objects on the table, asked everyone to join hands, and extinguished the candles. The room was plunged into complete darkness, but the objects on the table became visible from their slightly luminous glow. Andy slowly started to summon the non-existent spirit of Marie Ambrose.

The group was first asked to concentrate on the wicker ball. After a few minutes, it rose a few feet into the air, moved around the séance room, and gently returned to the table. Next, they turned their attention to the maraca, which, on a good night, slowly rolled across the table. These apparently ghostly phenomena were the result of the types of simple trickery that had been used by fake mediums at the turn of the century. It soon became obvious to us that they were still capable of having an impact on a modern-day audience. We filmed many of the séances with an infra-red camera, and the tapes showed that some people around the table gasped, some screamed, and many sat shaking in stony silence.

Then came the most important part of the evening: the suggestion. Andy asked Marie to make her presence known by moving the large, heavy table. The table remained completely stationary, but Andy suggested that it was levitating, using comments such as "That's good, Marie," "Lift the table higher," "The table is moving now." Andy then released the non-existent spirit of Marie back into the ether, the lights were turned on, and everyone was thanked for coming to the show.

Two weeks later, our guinea pigs were sent a questionnaire about their experiences during the show. We first asked people whether they thought that any of the events they had witnessed were actually paranormal. Forty percent of the people who expressed a prior belief in the paranormal thought that the phenomena were the result of genuine ghostly activity, compared with only about three percent of disbelievers. We then examined whether the suggestion had been effective. The results were startling. More than a third of people described how they had actually seen the table levitate. Again, participants' prior belief or disbelief in the paranormal played a key role, with half of disbelievers correctly stating that the table didn't move, versus just a third of believers. Our questionnaire also asked people whether they had had any unusual experiences during the séance. It seemed that the atmosphere we had created caused people to experience a whole range of spooky effects, with one in five reporting cold shivers, a strong sense of energy flowing through them, and a mysterious presence in the room.

Joseph Jastrow: Mind Doctor Extraordinaire

In January 2005 the London Science Museum invited me to stage an event examining the psychology of magic as part of The Magic Circle's Centenary celebrations. In preparation for the event, I tracked down two very early articles on the psychology of magic.

The first was written in 1896 by Joseph Jastrow (one of the founding fathers of American psychology) and published in the well-known academic journal *Science*. Jastrow is one of my academic heroes. He was an amazing character who conducted many unusual investigations, including one of the first experiments into subliminal perception, analyzing the dreams of blind people, and figuring out the psychology behind the Ouija board. Unfortunately, Jastrow also suffered from depression, with one Chicago newspaper reporting the onset of his illness with the headline, "Famous mind doctor loses his own."

In his 1896 article, Jastrow described how he had invited illusionists Alexander Herrmann and Harry Kellar to his laboratory at the University of Wisconsin and asked them to participate in a range of tests measuring their reaction time, speed of movement, memory, etc. Herrmann and Kellar were two of the most famous magicians of their day, and were locked in a constant battle of professional rivalry throughout most of their professional lives. If one made a donkey disappear, the other would make an elephant vanish. If one made a woman levitate above the stage, the other would have their assistant float a few feet higher. If one plucked a fan of cards from thin air, the other would perform the same feat blindfolded.

Jastrow noted that although both performers often claimed to possess remarkable psychological abilities, his results revealed little out of the ordinary. For example, Herrmann said that he possessed exceptional "at a glance abilities," claiming to be able to accurately observe and recall the contents of a shop window after just a fleeting look. Jastrow devised several tests of this ability, including, for example, briefly presenting Herrmann's with ten patches of cardboard, each of which had been cut into a different shape, and then asking him to remember as many of the shapes as possible. Herrmann's test results were remarkably similar to a control group of non-magicians, suggesting that Herrmann's claims to incredible "at a glance abilities" may have been more the result of puff than perception. Interestingly, Herrmann's results on many of the other tasks are quite strange, and it takes him several attempts before obtaining the types of scores that might be expected.

In a footnote to his paper, Jastrow accounts for this strangeness and provides an interesting insight into Hermann's personality, noting: "I feel it necessary to add that Mr. Herrmann perhaps did not do himself justice in some of the tests...often performing the tests in half the time taken by others. He...seemed confident of his ability to do what was required with little effort. It may well be that with a little more deliberation, and an opportunity of even a brief familiarity with the tests, better results would have been secured."

The first film of a magician

My research for the Science Museum event also uncovered a second article, published in the *Revue Philosophique* in 1894 by a French scientist named Alfred Binet, that proved more intriguing. Nowadays Alfred Binet is best known for two things. First, he established France's first psychology laboratory, and second, his work laid the foundations for modern day intelligence testing. However, Binet also had a strong interest in magic, and in his 1894 article contains his thoughts about the psychology behind prestidigitation.

It was, however, the final section of Binet's article that caught my attention. In it he describes how he conducted a unique analysis of sleight of hand in collaboration with the then famous Parisian photographer Georges Demeny and the French magician Raynaly. Demeny was a pioneer of "chronophotography"—a forerunner of modern day cinema that was devised to help analyze complicated sets of movements by taking several still photographs in rapid succession. The apparatus used for this work was extremely crude by today's standards. Demeny's camera was driven by a clockwork mechanism that quickly moved a very short strip of film (about twenty four frames long) past a relatively primitive lens at the rate of one frame every tenth of a second. This meant that Demeny could only record approximately two seconds of action and thus had to execute split-second timing to ensure that he captured the desired images. Demeny had achieved international fame by examining a wide range of human and animal movement—including, for example, analyzing birds in flight and dropping cats upside down from various heights to discover why they always landed on their feet. Binet's article described how Raynaly performed various tricks in front of Demeny's apparatus and that the resulting images were analyzed frame by frame to investigate the performer's sleight of hand abilities.

The images captured by Demeny were not reproduced in Binet's article, but were instead described as being "stored in laboratory records." I was curious. Did the images still exist? If so, they would be over a hundred and ten years old and had survived two world wars. Perhaps more importantly, they would constitute the first ever film of a magician. Historians often cite Robert Paul's 1896 footage of David Devant as the earliest film of a conjurer, but Demeny's film, made before 1894, would obviously predate the Devant footage by at least two years and thus qualify for the title. The search was on.

After a following several dead-ends, I contacted one of the world's most respected historians of early film, Professor Marta Braun from Toronto. Marta said that she hadn't ever come across the Binet images, but suggested that I contact Laurent Mannoni—an expert on Demeny and curator of an archive of early film at the French national library in Paris. After a long email exchange—*voilà*—Mannoni confirmed that three of Binet's "film" strips did indeed still exist, that they were stored in the archive, and that it was possible for me to gain access to them. A few weeks later I travelled to Paris and became the first psychologist to look at the images since Binet.

Laurent carefully led me into a darkened room lined with magic lanterns, projectors, and several props by the famous French magician Robert-Houdin. He walked over to one of the storage cabinets and carefully removed the three remaining "film" strips. The first strip contained just eleven images and showed Raynaly sitting on a chair in formal evening wear performing a card spring. The second strip also contained eleven images and showed a court card on the face of a deck changing to a spot card as Raynaly waves his hand over the card. However, the final strip was by far the most interesting. It contained twenty four images showing Raynaly dropping a ball from his left hand into his right, performing a fake transfer of the ball back into his left hand, and finally opening his hand to show the ball has vanished.

Laurent kindly gave me permission to make digital copies of the photographs, and by animating the images of the ball vanishing, it was possible to create a short film of Raynaly's performance. Although only a few seconds long, the film is the earliest known moving image of a magician—and unlike almost all other films of entertainers from around this period, it is based on images created for scientific research rather than public enjoyment. Watching the film is a remarkable experience. For a few brief moments it feels as if you have travelled back in time and are watching a remarkable performance that took place over a hundred years ago. I showed the film to magicians for the first time at an international conference on magic history, and Raynaly received his final, and much deserved, round of applause.

Afterwards a few people expressed slight frustration that the twenty-four images resulted in only a few seconds of footage. Binet, Demeny, and Raynaly seemed to have understood that most famous of show business sayings—always leave them wanting more.

Professor Richard Wiseman is a psychologist at the University of Hertfordshire in the UK, and co-author of Magic In Theory (University of Hertfordshire Press: UK), and Quirkology: The Curious Science of Everyday Life (MacMillan, UK). Binet's article, and a short animated film of the images, can be downloaded from: www.richardwiseman.com.

THE REAL JAMES RANDI
BY TIM CRIDLAND

James Randi is a retired magician who now makes his living fighting the paranormal. He is the author of books with titles like *Flim-Flam! The Truth about Unicorns, Parapsychology & Other Delusions.*

He paints a picture of himself as a crusader against paranormal nonsense, which he says is dangerous to the psyche. "I want to know what the difference between reality and fantasy is, and I want there to be a very sharp difference between the two with no overlap whatsoever," Randi stated in a self-taped interview. "I have accomplished that, quite nicely, in my personal life, and I try to pass that on to other people…"[1]

Although Randi may feel that he knows what reality is, a look at the past record reveals that some of what Randi is passing onto other people is not reality but a deception, the type of deception he is well versed in as a magician, and more importantly, as a self-promoter, and that his motivation is not truth, justice, and the American Way, but rather financial gain. Well, maybe that *is* the American Way.

Randi has had a colorful past, which he has repeatedly tried to reframe to suit his purpose. Randi has used various names over the years, some for professional reasons, and some for reasons that are unclear. He was born Randall James Hamilton Zwinge on Aug. 7, 1928, in Toronto, Canada.[2] He legally changed his name to James Randi in 1984.[3] He has used the names "Prince Ibis," "The Great Randall," "Randall the Telepath,"[4] and "Zo-Ran."[5] One legal paper lists such AKAs as "Adam Jersin," "Donald," and "Truth's Bodyguard."[6]

According to Randi, he has been fighting paranormal nonsense since he was a teenager. He claims that he was jailed briefly, when at the age of fifteen he burst on stage to denounce an exhibition at a Toronto spiritualist church as a simple magic trick, the old one-ahead system.[7, 8]

The problem is I have been unable to find Randi telling this story before the 1980s, coincidentally the same time that he was working on his book *The Faith Healers*,[9] which denounces just that type of chicanery.

If this account is true, Randi did not keep his anti-faith for long. At the age of 17, he dropped out of school and joined a traveling carnival, where he took on the persona of a fortune teller. He donned a turban and grew a goatee, used the name "Prince Ibis," and posed as a real psychic, both on stage[10] and in the media.[11] In later interviews Randi would state that it bothered him that people believed he was for real and he "... couldn't live that kind of lie."[12] Apparently, it did not bother him that much, because after leaving the carnival he printed up his first business card, which read "The Great Randall, Telepath."[13]

He toured with his phony psychic act for years. In one incarnation, he shows up in *The Toronto Evening Telegraph*, at age 22, fully representing himself as a genuine mind reader. On August 14, 1950, under the headline "Snoops on Minds," Randi, using the name Randall Zwinge, states that he first became aware that he had ESP when he was nine years old, and knew when the phone would ring. "I still sense when the phone is going to ring, but now I wait with my hands on it until it does ring." Randi made it clear that his powers are real, when he stated in a follow-up article, which ran in the August 28 issue of the same year, under the heading "He Sees the Future," that "Certain perceptions have been given me and I have improved them by deep study of the science of mental telepathy and clairvoyance."

Randi reproduced both of these articles in his book *The Magic of Uri Geller*; ostensibly to show how easy the media is fooled by phony psychics. He got out of the fraud business soon after this, he says incredibly, for fear of being worshiped: "I was to drop the entire pretense of being the real thing shortly after this run of articles appeared (there were dozens more), because I could not picture myself becoming a religious figure, as was bound to happen."[14]

He is obviously talking about these clippings, and others like them, in an audiotape that was intended for sale to magicians only, when he gave this advice to up-and-coming magicians:

"You have to be careful what statements you make, you have to be careful what you say and what you put in print, you have to be careful about the accomplishments that you set up, to go down in history as part of your past, because you may have to answer questions about those things one day or another.

"It would be very embarrassing for a reporter to come up with a clipping from the something-or-other newspaper and say 'how do you explain this?' if you don't have a reasonable explanation or excuse for it."[15]

Randi then assures the listener that he has always been able to explain his way out of this situation.

These historical accounts of Randi as a phony psychic are one 180 degrees at odds with what he now preaches, so Randi has to put what some people would call a "spin" or a "reframe" to change the perception of his past. Randi is a master propagandist, a skill no doubt learned from decades of self-promotion. Randi activates yet another retroactive motive to explain away another one of his former vocations: an astrologer for a trashy tabloid. In this case, he tries to pass it off as a social experiment. He brings up this fact about himself in his book *Flim-Flam*. Randi knows a propagandists tool: if there is dirt on you, bring it out yourself first. That way, you control the public's perception. Randi writes "Many years ago, when two friends of mine in Montreal, Canada, started a newspaper called *Midnight*, I was asked to write an astrological column for it. Had I any notion of what that newspaper would become, I would have run away screaming."[16] He then goes on to state that he saw this as a chance to conduct an experiment, that he cut up old astrology magazines and pasted them back together at random for his column, which ran under the pseudonym Zo-ran. The results were that people accepted what he "wrote" without question, apparently accepting him as an authority figure. Seeing this, he got out of the astrology business. He states that he was "…only seventeen at the time…"[17] when all of this happened.

There are lots of problems with Randi's account. *Midnight* would go on to become the supermarket tabloid *The Globe*, and in doing so, actually got less sensational and sleazy. The first few issues had headlines like "Montreal's Unsolved Murders" and "McGill Students Hold Sex Orgies,"[18] so Randi knew just what type of "newspaper" he was writing for. But what really gives Randi away is that the first issue of *Midnight* came out in November of 1954.[19] Randi was born in 1928 and would have been 26 when that first issue came out, not 17. Could this be an honest mistake? Although some biographies state that Randi did spend time in Montreal when he was 17 or so [20] (when he was Prince Ibis, remember), think back to events in your life that happened when you were 17 and when you were 26, then ask yourself if you could confuse these very different times in your life.

Randi's involvement with *Midnight* mostly likely happened when he was a performer in the city's many nightclubs. Montreal had become an entertainment mecca during Prohibition, when people from New York would take a trip north of the border where booze was still legal. When prohibition ended, Montreal's nightlife continued and it is still renowned to this day.

Midnight was started partly to cover Montreal's nightlife, its publishers being fixtures on the nightclub scene. At the time, Montreal's nightclubs were controlled by the Cotroni crime family.[21] *Midnight*'s libertine publisher Joe Azaria rubbed elbows with these underworld figures often: "We used to get together. They didn't talk to me about their business and I didn't talk to them about mine."[22] This time in Montreal must have included some of the most interesting stories of Randi's life. Randi seems much more closely tied to *Midnight* than he would care to admit. The earliest issue of *Midnight* that I could find at the Quebec Bibliothèque Nationale (Feb. 18, 1956, headline: "Sex-Cops Raid Three Brothels Nab 17 Inmates") has Randi's name on the front cover art. When Randi was a fixture at the Quebec nightclubs, his act had expanded to include escapes,[23] hypnosis[24] (something else he would later decry), and plain old stage magic. The stage magic and escapes eventually got him over the U.S. border, earning him appearances on the children's TV show *Wonderama*.[25]

Randi made his way from Canada to the U.S. in the late 1950s. By this time he had dropped all of his phony psychic and astrologer routines, but he was still not an outright foe of the paranormal. Randi became a "regular" on the Long John Nebel Show,[26] a late-night radio show on New York City's WOR that was considered by many to be "a somewhat skeptical version of today's Art Bell [show]."[27]

Nebel made his mark by interviewing people who claimed that they had been given rides to Venus on flying saucers, or who believed that there was a race of people living under the earth who tormented surface dwellers with rays. Long John considered Randi "one of the few people as skeptical as I am,"[28] yet neither one was completely closed to the idea of the paranormal, at least not yet. In fact, Long John's book *Way Out World* describes an on-the-air ESP experiment that took place on January 15, 1960, for which Randi could offer no explanation. The usually skeptical Long John wrote "…for once in my life I didn't say 'I don't buy it.' I just sat there and wondered."[29]

As it turned out, Long John got an offer for more money from another station and left, and James Randi took over the spot at WOR.[30] Randi was now in direct competition with Nebel.[31] Randi's show would sometimes cover the "way out" topics that Nebel was known for. Jim Moseley, publisher of *Saucer News*, was a regular guest on Randi's show and a friend during the mid-1960s. Moseley wrote: "At the time, Randi was relatively open-minded about saucers and other weirdness."[32] Randi would eventually buy a house in Rumson, NJ, with profits from the radio show.[33]

In fact Randi was also a regular at Moseley's flying-saucer meetings and conventions.[34] He made an appearance at Moseley's most infamous flying saucer convention in June of 1967. Randi was on the bill with people like Rev. Frank Stranges, "The Flying Saucer Evangelist" who claimed to know a man from Venus. In his lecture Randi was quoted as saying "Let's not fool ourselves. There are some garden variety liars involved in all this. But in among all the trash and nonsense perpetrated in the name of Ufology, I think there is a small grain of truth."[35]

I can imagine how such a statement would go over with Randi's followers today, and how they would react to finding out that Randi's radio show had guests like Timothy Green Beckley,[36] aka "Mr. UFO," and Gray Barker,[37] who more than anyone popularized the legend of the Men In Black.

So when did Randi really start his crusade against the paranormal and nonsense thinking? It all revolves around—you guessed it—Uri Geller.

Uri Geller, the superstar psychic, fascinated the U.S. in the early 1970s. I leave it to you to decide what Geller really is, but it cannot be disputed that, real or not, he is very good at what he does. He made the cover of scores of magazines and appeared on many TV shows when he first came to the U.S. from Israel. And riding on this wave of publicity was James Randi,[38] reinvented as the crusader against nonsense, and all in the name of truth. This was the first time that Randi got continuing major national press, and it can be said that if it were not for Geller, Randi would not be where he is today, words Randi hates to hear.

Randi followed Geller onto TV shows and then wrote a book,[39] with the intention of putting Geller out of business.

He invited Geller to sue him[40] and got his wish.

Geller sued Randi and CSICOP, an organization that Randi helped found, with mixed results.[41] Geller was successful in having false information removed from future editions of Randi's anti-Geller book, but Randi is the master of the spin, so according to him, he lost no suits at all, causing author Robert Anton Wilson to remark that Randi lost the court case but won the war of the press releases.

One case that seems cut and dried is a lawsuit that Geller won against Randi in Japan. In an interview with a Japanese magazine, Randi called Geller a sociopath and said that Geller had caused a scientist to commit suicide after the scientist had found out that Geller had tricked him. The scientist's death certificate said that he died of natural causes, so Geller easily won a judgment.[42] You would think that Randi would

THE REAL JAMES RANDI   165

fess up to this one and admit that he had wronged Geller, but he hasn't. Randi says that it is all a misunderstanding over a poor translation. He claims he was speaking metaphorically when he said the scientist "shot himself in the head," but the translator did not understand,[43] and that if he had been able to travel to Japan, he would have won, and besides, Geller did not collect the money anyway, having agreed to not pursue it as part of an out-of-court settlement of another legal case.[44]

But Randi had made a similar statement, years before the Japanese interview, to Canadian reporter Patricia Owen: "One scientist, a metallurgist, wrote a paper backing Geller's claim that he could bend metal. The scientist shot himself after I showed him how the key bending trick was done."[45] In an even earlier interview, Randi said that the death was "…under conditions described as not natural."[46]

The most embarrassing lawsuit was brought by Eldon Byrd, a scientist who was favorable to Geller. After the appearance of some anonymously mailed audiotapes, Randi accused Byrd of, among other things, being responsible for a "blackmail campaign" against him. The accusation was printed in a magazine interview and Byrd sued for libel. The tape's contents were embarrassing to Randi, but it seems tame today, after all of the "celebrities at their worst" tapes and stolen celebrity sex tapes that have circulated and even been sold commercially. The tape's contents had nothing to do with the paranormal, but what is noteworthy is the elaborate spin Randi put on the situation. He sent out a few communications trying to explain the whole thing, saying "My own lawyer, at my insistence, asked that the entire tape be played for the courtroom and jury, so that the true nature of the record would be understood, instead of being misrepresented as it usually was…"[47] And in a an email, he stated: "The jury heard the 'tape'—at my insistence…"[48] In fact, the court transcript showed just the opposite, that Randi's lawyer did everything she could to stop the tape from being played, and that the judge in the case found Randi's statement of how the tape was made incredible, saying to Randi's lawyer "…it is possible that your client told this Court, this jury, and the New York Skeptics a bald face lie."[49]

The result of the trial was an embarrassment to all involved. Randi lost the case, Byrd got no monetary judgment, and both of their private lives were all over the papers. Despite all of this, Randi considers these cases wins for him.

One of Randi's biggest publicity gimmicks is his offer of a cash prize for proof of the paranormal. It seems hard to imagine that he would ever pay it out, not only because to do so would negate his created persona, but who really believes that the judgment of truth comes from James Randi? Only the most gullible believe the offer is legitimate. Randi as much as admitted it was false when he told his then friend, astronomer Dennis Rawlins, that in regards to the challenge, "I always have an out."[50] Randi has tried to wiggle out of the statement over the years, but has never denied it. The word "out" is well known to magicians. It means a way of recovering if a trick doesn't go as you planned.[51] And what happens to the unwinnable prize money? I don't know about now, but in 1981, when it was just $10,000, Randi bragged "I pay my mortgage with the interest."[52]

Randi has come a long way since he first started touring with a carnival sideshow, and he has used a lot of "outs" to get there. He won a MacArthur genius award. A multi-millionaire paid for a foundation with his name on it that will live on after his death. He has had an asteroid named after him. He seems to have a cult of personality around him; devoted fans create conventions around him in Las Vegas and patrol internet sites to fight negative comments about him. He really is an interesting guy who has had an interesting life.

So why do I bring up all of this? Because this is what Randi demands we do to others, because Randi himself is promoting a socio/spiritual viewpoint which he says is the best and that we can all aspire to; and to show that, just like any other true believer, Randi will distort the truth in order to protect "the cause," that his followers will aid him in this, and like many other personalities associated with a cause, it is really about putting personal gain above philosophical and scientific truth.

References

1. Randi, *From Beyond Understanding* [cassette tape] (Martin Breese Productions, London, UK 1977/1980) [recorded Dec. 1976].
2. "James Randi," *Newsmakers 1990*, Issue 2, Gale Research, 1990.
3. "James Randi," *Contemporary Authors Online*, Gale 2008.
4. These names are cited by Randi in numerous biographies and interviews
5. James Randi, *Flim–Flam!: The Truth about Unicorns, Parapsychology & Other Delusions* (Lippincott & Crowell 1980) p.62.
6. *Uri Geller v. James Randi* (No. 93-7140, United States Court of Appeals for The District of Columbia).
7. Philip Yam, "A Skeptically Inquiring Mind," *Scientific American*, July 1995 p.34.
8. Richard Pyratt, USA Today (Aug. 29, 1986), quoted in "James Randi," *Encyclopedia of Occultism and Parapsychology*, (5th Edition, Gale Group 2001).
9. James Randi, *The Faith Healers* (Prometheus, NY, 1987)

10. Numerous biographies and interviews.
11. Michael Shermer, "An Amazing Life" [interview] *Skeptic*, Vol.8, No.4 2001 p.36.
12. Scot Morris, "James Randi," [interview] *Omni*, April 1980 p.77.
13. Randi, *From Beyond...* Op. cited
14. James Randi, *The Magic of Uri Geller*, (Ballantine Books, New York, 1975) p.262.
15. Randi, *From Beyond...* Op. cited
16. James Randi, *Flim-Flam* Op. cited p.61.
17. James Randi, *Flim-Flam* Op. cited p.62.
18. Bill Sloan, *I Watched a Wild Hog Eat My Baby*, (Prometheus Books, 2001) p.57.
19. Bill Sloan, Op. cited p.57.
20. Owen, "The Amazing Randi" *Toronto Star*, Aug. 23, 1986 p.M1.
21. Peter Edwards, *Blood Brothers: How Canada's Most Powerful Mafia Family Runs Its Business*, (Seal Books, Toronto, 1990).
22. Alan Hustak, "Publisher Got Rich with His Tabloid Empire," *Montreal Gazette*, Aug. 19, 1990.
23. "Stunts For Fund," *Chicago Tribune*, Feb. 20, 1957 p.2
24. Walter Gibson, *The Key to Hypnotism* (Key Publishing Company, New York, 1956) [contains numerous photos of Randi's Hypnosis act].
25. James Randi, on *Internet Movie Data Base* (www.imdb.com) [Wonderama started in 1955].
26. Long John Nebel, *Way Out World* (Prentice Hall 1961) p.201.
27. James W. Moseley, *Shockingly Close to the Truth* (Prometheus Books 2002) p.122.
28. Long John Nebel, Op. cited p.212
29. Long John Nebel, Op. cited pp.210-213
30. The Amazing Randi Show on WOR ran from late 1964-early 1966.
31. James W. Moseley, Op. cited p.189
32. James W. Moseley, Op. cited p.189
33. Michael Shermer, Op. cited p.37
34. James W. Moseley, Op. cited p.18
35. Willard Clopton, "Air Force's UFO Expert Meets the Man From S.A.U.C.E.R.S." *Washington Post*, June 27, 1967.
36. "Radio," *New York Times*, Jan. 30, 1965 p. 55.
37. James W. Moseley, Op cited, p.190.
38. Scot, Morris, Op. cited p.104.
39. James Randi, *The Magic of...* Op. cited.
40. Randi, *From Beyond...* Op. cited
41. Marcello Truzzi, "An End to the Uri Geller vs. Randi & CSICOP Litigations?," *PSI Researcher*, Society for Psychical Research.
42. Marcello Truzzi, Op. cited
43. An article in the Aug. 16, 1964 *Bridgeport Post* says that Randi "...is able to do his act in Japanese."

44. Carol Krol, "Cuckoos and Cocoa Puffs," *The Skeptical Eye*, Vol. 8 No. 3 1995.
45. Patricia Owen, "The Amazing Randi" *Toronto Star*, Aug. 23, 1986.
46. Scot Morris, Op. cited p.108.
47. James Randi, *Position Statement*, April 1999, quoted in *Saucer Smear* Sept. 1, 1999.
48. James Randi, *Action initiated...*, Dec. 4, 1996, email from Randi Hotline
49. *Eldon Byrd vs. James Randi et al* [trial transcript], May 26th, 1993, quoted in *Saucer Smear*, Nov. 5, 1999
50. Dennis Rawlins, "sTarbaby," *Fate Magazine*, Oct. 1981
51. Charles H. Hopkins, *"Outs" Precautions and Challenges*, (Charles H. Hopkins & Co., Philadelphia, PA 1940).
52. Kay Barlett, "Amazing Randi," *Associated Press*, reproduced in *Pacific Stars and Stripes*, June 1, 1981.

***Tim Cridland** is perhaps better known as Zamora the Torture King, the name under which he performs in Las Vegas. Originally a member of The Jim Rose Sideshow Circus, his stunts include fire eating, sword swallowing, body skewering, and self-electrification. Zamora co-authored (with Jan Gregor),* Circus of the Scars: The True Inside Odyssey of a Modern Circus Sideshow, *a history of the Jim Rose Circus Sideshow, and (with Joe Oesterle)* Weird Las Vegas and Nevada: Your Alternative Travel Guide to Sin City and the Silver State.

Don't Miss Our Previous Issues...

The Anomalist 13:
INTERMEDIATE STATES

The Anomalist 12:
THE UNIVERSE WANTS TO PLAY

Available from Amazon, Barnes & Noble,
or your local bookstore. For more information about the contents
of each issue, visit AnomalistBooks.com.